Most church leade

hemorrhaging of young adults from the church. The stats are terri
fying, and the picture is bleak. So, what's the hope for the future?
The hope must be for a move of the Spirit that revitalizes faith in
the emerging generations. This hope should drive us to our knees in
prayer, but it should equally lift us to our feet, ready for action. This
book is a rallying cry for the church to establish intimate communities that take seriously the spiritual formation of our young people in
an extremely challenging cultural moment, so they can carry the fire
of God when it falls. If you care about young adults and the renewal
of the church, do whatever it takes to get a copy this brilliant book.

—Pete Hughes

Lead Pastor, Kings Cross Church, and Author of *All Things New*

What makes this book different is that Austin is not talking *about*
emerging generations, he's talking as *part* of the demographic that
he is also looking to serve. This perspective is invaluable to peers,
parents, and seasoned leaders alike. He also isn't talking theology
or offering bright ideas without hard-won practice on the ground.
I appreciate Austin's depth and insight and academic gifting, but
it is his personal and compassionate voice as a pastor and friend—
currently living the very things he is writing—that makes this work
so powerful. All of us seeking to see God turn the tide of faith in
Jesus and belonging in his church should read this and be ready to
apply its wisdom.

—Miriam Swanson

Fusion USA Director

In a culture where consumerism models our approach to church,
Austin Wofford gives an alternative, more kingdom-minded
approach. This book invites you to engage the next generation in a
way that fights against the statistics of losing them.

—Rev. Mark Swayze

Next Gen Pastor at The Woodlands Methodist Church

There's a viral article every week about something this generation of young adults has ruined, but in *Forged,* Austin Wofford has written a compelling counternarrative about young adults that reimagines them as a catalyst for renewal in the church. As someone who spent my first six years of ministry working with twenty-somethings, I couldn't agree more. If you're tired of seeing young adults as a problem to be solved and ready to see them as potential to unleash, read this book.

—Austin Gohn
Pastor and Author of *A Restless Age: How Saint Augustine Helps You Make Sense of Your Twenties*

Someone once said, "If you truly listen to people, they will tell you how to lead them to Jesus Christ." In *Forged,* that's exactly what Austin Wofford has done. Rooted in his wealth of personal experience and wide-ranging research, he has listened carefully to today's emerging adults and understands their profound heart-cry for relationship, family, and a new way of being church. Everyone who cares about reaching today's emerging adults should read this book.

—Stephen Seamands
Professor Emeritus of Christian Doctrine
Asbury Theological Seminary

As beings created from and for community, we have always longed for ways to articulate the elemental truths Austin lays out in this important undertaking, and he has finally given us the language. *Forged* is not merely a clever, addicting, and profoundly written book, I believe it is the manual on how to do community the authentic way. The kingdom way. *Forged* is not for a specific age group, although it is about one, and I know the timeless truths underscored in these pages will highly resonate with everyone.

—Reward Sibanda
Pastor of Engagement at UPPERROOM Dallas

Whenever a human body is hemorrhaging, one of the first things you want to do is get an accurate diagnosis of why blood is leaving the body. Such is the case of young adults leaving the church today. One of my favorite insights from Austin is this diagnosis, and he does it with metaphor and image that make it convincing, compelling, and meaningful. He exhibits an uncanny ability to state with clarity the cultural narrative(s) infecting the hearts and minds of young adults, leaving many bereft of a faith community that could cultivate in them a vibrant life with God. But Austin doesn't leave us with just a diagnosis. He is, at heart, a pastoral practitioner and the richness of this text is reading about the real-world response that he and his wife, along with a team of committed others, are forging that takes its cues from the dynamics of the early church in the book of Acts. Not only will you want to read this book, you will also want to keep an eye on what is percolating among them as its embodiment.

—Chris Kiesling
Professor of Discipleship and Human Development
Asbury Theological Seminary

Many of us realize that we are at a whatever-it-takes moment when it comes to emerging adults in our churches and families. We know that we can no longer stand by and continue hemorrhaging them away as they suffer in isolation. Yet so much of the time, we hardly know where to start. Austin Wofford points us toward deeper understanding and faithful, strategic response. And he should know as an emerging leader himself with experience in the trenches of engaging his generation. *Forged* is a must-read for pastors, campus ministry leaders, parents and grandparents, and anyone sharing hope for a new move of God's grace in our day.

—David Thomas
New Room Conference
Alpha USA

The religious landscape in North America has radically changed over the last several decades. The fastest growing religious group in North America is the religious "nones"—young-adults who are disavowing religion all together. More than ever before, we need guides to help us understand how to reach the next generation with the timeless gospel of Jesus Christ. In *Forged*, Austin Wofford has written a timely book that will help church leaders create discipleship communities that will reach young adults and bring renewal to the church.

—Winfield Bevins
Director of Church Planting at Asbury Theological Seminary
Author of *Liturgical Mission: The Work of the People for the Sake of the World*

FORGED

Young Adults
and the Renewal
of the Church

Austin Wofford

Printed in the United States of America

Cover design by Strange Last Name
Page design and layout by PerfecType, Nashville, Tennessee

Wofford, Austin.
    Forged : young adults and the renewal of the church / Austin Wofford. – Franklin, Tennessee : Seedbed Publishing, ©2022.

        pages ; cm.

        Includes bibliographical references.
        ISBN: 9781628249484 (paperback)
        ISBN: 9781628249491 (mobi)
        ISBN: 9781628249507 (epub)
        ISBN: 9781628249514 (pdf)
        OCLC: 1334914228

        1. Church work with young adults. 2. Young adults--Religious life--United States. 3. Young adults--United Sates--Social life and customs--21st century. 4. Church renewal   I. Title.

BV4446.W63 2022   268.434   2022942428

SEEDBED PUBLISHING
Franklin, Tennessee
seedbed.com

To the Gulletts, whose open front door
has welcomed many sojourners home.

CONTENTS

FOREWORD

*Experimental groups seeking to engage the Christian faith
in a postmodern context will often lack the resources,
profile or success record of the Boomer congregations. By
definition, they are new, untried, relatively disorganized
and fearful of self-promotion. They reject the corporate
model of their Boomer forebears and thus do not appear,
according to existing paradigms, to be significant. But don't
be fooled. Somewhere in the genesis and genius of these
groups, is hidden the future of Western Christianity. To
dismiss them is to throw away the seeds of our survival.*
—Gerald Kelly

THERE IS SOMETHING SO SIMPLE ABOUT GOING BACK
to the future. By foraging back in the ancient text, we still find
jewels of truth that have the power to transform individuals,
families, and communities.

Austin Wofford has embraced humble boldness. It is always
so much easier to remain within the comfortable and the predict-
able. It takes Joshua-like strength and courage to dare to consider
a move across the river to the road less travelled.

The statistics of the church emptying of the millennial and
Gen Z are now commonly known. Yet foolishness requires us
to "do the same old thing, in the same way and expect different
results."

Is it possible to have the good, old-fashioned guts to move from the safe into the realm of the prophetic, to believe that God can use us like David "to serve the purpose of God in his generation."

The advent of this warfare requires a different battle strategy, using different weapons, mobilizing a different army, expecting different results. Austin is calling the body to reconsider the mission of the church for the decades which lie ahead of us. He does not have an axe to grind but a vision to impart. Stirred by the possibility of what this global gospel community could look like, it empowers him to dare, to risk, to call his community, as well as us dear readers, to prayerfully consider a new/old way.

This kind of boldness can wrestle with that space where ideation and function meet together. Throwing a vision down the road for us to follow does not mean it will end up looking exactly as he describes. There are many questions yet to be discovered, never mind be answered. Failure along the way is inevitable. Yet the conviction of his narrative makes these potholes worth stumbling through.

Read, reflect, rest, and then, in faith, consider the obedience to the higher call that he is inviting us into.

Along the way we will all discover new ways for "his ways are not our ways."

This is a book worth reading, for it enables discovery en route.

Chris Wienand
Founder of the Genesis Collective
Pastor of Genesis Costa Mesa

INTRODUCTION

The spiritual crisis overtaking the West is the most serious since the fall of the Roman Empire in the fifth century. The light of Christianity is flickering out all over the Western Hemisphere. There are people alive today who may live to see the death of Christianity.
—Pope Emeritus Benedict XVI[1]

MILLENNIALS AND GEN ZERS ARE LEAVING THE Christian faith by the millions. Studies show that a gap between young adults and the church exists and it is widening. The Pinetops Foundation recently reported in "The Great Opportunity" that if trends continue, then more than one million youth in the American church today will choose to leave each year for the next three decades. Between twenty to forty million youth raised in families that call themselves Christians are projected to no longer claim Christ by the year 2050.[2]

This young adult exodus from the church is a big problem. American Christianity is in the midst of a precipitous fall that may determine the state of the church for the next century. It is time to sound the alarm and to address the seismic religious earthquake taking place in emerging generations.

As church leaders, the separation between Jesus and our young adults registers deep within our spirits. Studies like the one mentioned are not just statistics for us. We do not carelessly watch twenty-somethings walk out of the church doors, never to return.

The emerging adult exodus is more personal than that. Most of us have painful stories of loved ones who are part of this church exodus. Their absence leaves a vacuum both in our communities and in our hearts.

The Heart-Cry of Belonging

A decade of campus ministry has given me the chance to walk alongside hundreds of Millennial and Gen Z Christians. I have prayed, worshipped, and talked with young adults on dozens of university campuses from across the country over the past few years. These students have opened my eyes and ears to the hopes, struggles, fears, and desires of people thirty-five and under.

These relationally bankrupt generations long to be known. And many of them are confused why this need is not met in their local church. Over and over I hear young adults tell me things like: "I go every Sunday, but I do not know anyone in the church"; "My anxiety was so bad that I could not get out of bed this morning"; "Pray for me. I want to follow Jesus, but I don't have anyone to encourage me in my faith"; "I am so depressed that I cannot feel God"; or "I need spiritual friends to hold me accountable, but I do not know where to find them. Do you know anybody?"

Churches have given them plenty of options to *observe* worship by consuming digital content or by attending a seamless Sunday-morning service, but young adults are confused why their church experience stops with observation. They are looking for communities where they belong, participate, and are known. Unsatisfied and restless, many search for a faith community that will allow them to step beyond church *observation* and into church *participation*.

Belonging is the heart-cry of the Millennial and Gen Z generations. This is because they live in the fallout of expressive individualism—the unending quest for freedom and choice. This ethos eats away at emerging adults. They are constantly transitioning jobs, cities, schools, and careers. Their friendships are now managed online and on phones. They struggle to bond with others as they try to establish their adult lives. Twenty-somethings are victim to the ideals of expressive individualism and have become lonely, disconnected, and relationally stunted as a result.

They understand that the relationships offered to them on a daily basis are shallow, and they want their church to present a redemptive alternative. Their desire is for church to be the place where they experience the real meat of life—intimacy with God and others. They want to laugh, cry, celebrate, and mourn together, and to know and be known by other believers. They want to move from church *attendance* to church *belonging*.

Digital Farmer

Over the last couple of years, my wife, Maddie, and I felt a growing call to plant a house church network. We announced to our friends and family in March of 2020 that we were going to finally pursue the dream. In the five days following the announcement, COVID went from Wuhan to Seattle, and then from Seattle to my neighborhood. All churches were immediately shut down and the only way to worship was in the home. It was like God said, "I'm glad you prefer to plant in homes, because it's your only option."

COVID provided plenty of obstacles to starting a house church movement in 2020, but I remember having a conversation with one would-be church-planting expert who didn't like the idea under any circumstance, good or bad. He told me: "No. Don't start your church in homes. You'll never make it. Launch large. Then cut big. Shoot for a thousand people on your first Sunday. You want to create an audience. This will be your base of givers. A church will never succeed without starting with a substantially sized audience of people."

I gave a small amount of pushback: "We want to plant a church where believers gather in their own homes to worship God, forge Christian family, and reach their neighborhoods through missional living. Our desire is to start with small groups of deeply discipled Christians, and to grow by engaging the unchurched."

The church-planting coach didn't mince words when shooting down my idealism: "People don't want to be in the home. Most want to remain anonymous in church. The majority just need a service that they can attend easily and then leave."

"What about transfer growth," I asked? "I don't want to have the next 'cool church,' only to grow with believers from other churches."

His response: "Don't worry about people who come from other churches. They didn't belong in those churches in the first place. Just don't start in the home. You need a large audience that acts as a base of givers. Collect a crowd from the start and then use the donor base however you need. That's key to being sustainable. A large Sunday service is your only realistic chance of impacting your city."

I thanked the coach for his honesty, said goodbye, and hung up the phone. I wasn't discouraged or surprised. I've been in the consumer Christian context long enough to know its attitudes and talking points—and to know that it's largely ineffective in reaching and forming emerging generations.

You can see the values of expressive individualism in the comments from this church-planting coach. He represents a low-commitment and consumer-friendly model of religion to which America has grown accustomed. This easy-come/easy-go brand of church is prevalent. Emerging adults are choosing the easy-go option, and the pandemic has exacerbated this effect.

COVID forced churches into a digital streaming gold rush. Some have gone so far as to launch phone apps that double as a church campus. These applications aim to replace physical churches with video streaming. You can now attend church on your phone, tablet, or computer.

Viewers can "attend" a digital worship service from wherever they like; stay in the bed and log on to church, watch church from a coffee shop, or go to the grocery store and listen in. The app attempts to replace different aspects of a physical church through digital means. You can "meet" people in a digital "lobby," sing along with worship, and watch the sermon. However, there is no physical body-to-body relationship with other people, and these digital-driven churches mistakenly reduce church to the act of online content consumption.

COVID has accelerated the growth of this online consumeristic model. Pastors are now forced to be digital farmers, attempting to harvest the screen-time attention of young adults. The church's pivot toward digital content will become more prevalent as our society becomes increasingly digitized and individualized. This is celebrated by some, but the big problem persists: we are losing roughly one million Millennial and Gen Z men and women every year.

Hunger for Renewal

It is time for a different strategy. As pastors, leaders, elders, parents, and committed Christians, we see the problem and feel prodded to make a change. We can no longer do church as normal. We want to stand in the gap and contend for renewal. We hunger to see a fresh move of God sweep across our society and to sweep up the next generation in the process. We don't just believe that God could reach Millennials and Gen Zers, we feel that he must.

Yet, we do not feel equipped to lead into the next revival. The gap between church and culture feels too wide. The lifestyle of young adults has progressed too rapidly to keep up. The new life stage of emerging adulthood is a mystery to many of us.

Connecting with this age group is a matter of survival for our faith traditions, but we struggle to understand the people we are most desperate to reach. This gap has placed a deep-seated anxiety within us. We want to take action, but feel stuck in confusion.

That is why my hope for this book is twofold. First, I want to help readers see emerging adults with clarity. They are experiencing their late teens and twenties unlike any generation in the past. I want us to become familiar with their aches, struggles, hopes, lifestyle, and spirituality so we can empathize with them and lead them in confidence.

Second, I want us to fall in love with a point of renewal that we cannot miss as church leaders and committed disciples of Jesus. That point of renewal is family-like community within emerging generations. We have only begun in this introduction to uncover the damage done by expressive individualism, and a return to early-church community is our only hope of reversing its effect.

The premise of this book is simple: if we can wield the power of intimate community, then renewal could be right around the corner.

Forged Family

David Brooks once used the term *forged family* to reference communities of individuals that bond together as family in a shared struggle for survival.[3] The term immediately struck me as important for emerging generational ministry. When someone forges metal, they bring two independent metal objects into an intense fire. This fire welds the two separate metal pieces together, making them into one object.

Twenty-somethings are isolated and each of them is in the fire of identity formation. The journey of becoming an established adult will put their understanding of God through a blue-hot fire.

Too many of them go through that fire alone, and their faith burns up in the process.

But we can help build communities of young adults who go through the fire together. Give them a vision for a shared life with God, and they will weld together in the flame and be formed into the likeness of Jesus.

We are not referring to blood relatives when we use the term *family*. We mean the family of God—the brothers and sisters of Jesus—the children of our heavenly Father. Forged families happen anywhere young adults come together in intimate community to support one another in the emerging adult fire of life and faith.

Forged family is more of an idea or concept than it is a rigid structure. I am not presenting a precise model or a quick-fix system. Also, this book is not an attempt to advocate for house churches. I lead a house church movement but am not a house church purist. I am thankful for churches large and small, traditional and contemporary, rural and urban, and profoundly believe that God will use all makes and models to reach Millennials and Gen Zers.

This means that we can use the forged-family principles in this book to establish meaningful young-adult communities within our churches, regardless of tradition or background. Forged families can exist in any community where Jesus followers rely on each other in noncasual and family-like ways.

Part One of this book tackles the community struggles of emerging adulthood. The first chapter gives us the wide-lens view of the impact of individualism and the breakdown of relationships in young adults. Chapters 2 through 5 name the specific idols and barriers that block these young people from Christian community and from each other.

In Part Two, we will learn the ways in which the church can form community with emerging generations. Chapters 6 through 10 will detail how the church can become their relational hub and explore five different movements that we can make together to forge family.

Renewal in emerging generations will not be far off if we can capture the power of intimate relationship. My prayer is that, by the end of this book, readers will feel equipped to forge family with emerging adults in their lives. I'm looking forward to taking this journey into community together.

PART ONE

CHAPTER ONE

The Wall of Identity
Building Yourself from Scratch

*This life has shown me how we're
mended and how we're torn.
How it's okay to be lonely as long as you're free.*
—Rich Mullins, "Elijah"

"I'M STILL A CHRISTIAN, BUT I JUST CAN'T DO CHURCH anymore."

"I'm exploring other religions."

"I just need a break from worship for a while."

"I'm spiritual but not religious."

"I need to discover who I am apart from my Christian background."

How many times have we heard these phrases from twenty-somethings over a cup of coffee, a shared meal, or a social media post? My heart sinks each time these words have left the mouth of a friend. They are spoken with (many times) untold backstories of hurt, pain, or confusion, and they have the power to land on any Christian leader with deadly force. These hallmark phrases of faith deconstruction accompany too many young adults through that stage of life.

It's easy to feel helpless when struck by the words of deconstruction. Christian leaders are tempted to hear them as personal failure. The words are especially hard to stomach when spoken by someone within our faith community. Many of us have seen emerging adult communities within our churches fall apart or dissolve because of similar words or conflicts. Twenty-somethings' relationships with their churches can feel as fragile as their relationships with one another. They seem to always be on the edge of breaking away.

What if I told you that young adult relationship difficulty and their faith deconstruction were closely linked problems? What if I told you that robust family-like Christian communities would help them maintain their faith through their twenties? You want to hear these phrases less and to see new Christians made and formed within their generations. That's why it is important to understand the wall of identity.

A person's twenties act as a growth stage for identity-making in adulthood. Most people don't come into their first job, first home, or new marriage with a concrete sense of who they are as an adult. Emerging adulthood is a journey of setting that identity.

The wall of identity blocks people from the church and from one another. This is the first of five walls in the chapters ahead that will give us an inside look at why it's so difficult for young adults to find homes in the church and community in general.

This wall comes first because it is so fundamental to young adulthood. This chapter will work as an overview of the life stage and the journey of identity formation within it. We will see that Gen Zers and Millennials struggle emotionally, relationally, and spiritually. It will also become obvious that these struggles are intertwined with the wall of identity.

Without understanding the wall of identity, we are hopeless to break through any of the five walls. But the leader who can see through this wall can break through and take emerging adults in their Christian communities along with them.

Starting at Rock Bottom

The first step toward understanding the wall of identity is to empathize with today's emerging adults. To do that, we will need to connect with our experience in that life stage. Could I entice you with a thought exercise? I think it would be fun to connect with the twenty-three-year-old inside of you.

Take a second to remember your life at twenty-three. (This will be harder for some of us than others!) What was your living situation like? Who did you room with? What car did you drive? Had you found love yet? Where was your career? How were the numbers in your bank account? Were you steady and assured in life or were you experiencing a fluid and uncertain time?

My guess is that most of us remember our twenties with a smile, knowing that we had way more questions about life than we had answers.

I can't help but laugh when remembering my twenty-third year of life. A specific instance sticks out in my mind that epitomizes my early twenties. It was the morning that the heat in my car died. I pressed my hands together and shook all over. It was seven o'clock on a cold winter morning in early February. I just couldn't seem to get warm. A biting cold pierced through my jacket as I waited for the car to heat. I sat there alone, shivering, and itching.

I shivered from the frosty morning weather, but the itching was the result of a mysterious skin disease. My stumped doctor had misdiagnosed this disease for months. He was frustrated and at the end of his rope, and suggested that I was hallucinating my symptoms. This turned out to be a misdiagnosis but, nevertheless, I sat in my frigid car that morning and wondered if my itching was caused by insanity. Desperation washed over me as I considered how life had become so miserable.

This was the morning that felt like rock bottom. I had graduated college just six months earlier. In college I had friends, happiness, and fulfillment, but the half year since graduation ushered abundant change and hardship into my life.

I walked out of college and into adulthood unaware of what I was about to face, and I found myself blindsided by the transition into the real world. I was knocked over as nearly everything went wrong those first few months. I moved to a city where I knew only a couple of people, started a new job (where I fundraised my own salary), had my heart broken by a girl, suffered from an undiagnosed skin disease, and now discovered the heat in my car was broken. The six months between graduation and that cold February morning had been the toughest in my life.

I didn't visualize that adulthood would start like this. Graduation was supposed to launch me into freedom and satisfaction. You are, after all, promised your best life after college; you earn an adult-sized income, find true love, travel the world, and build a career that is impressive and purposeful . . . or so I thought. These dreams eluded me. I was, instead, living a broke, sick, and lonely nightmare! Life had not gone as planned.

Sometimes I look back on that February morning in the car and it serves as a reminder of where I started out in my adulthood. It was a tough time but, thankfully, it didn't last forever. My circumstances transformed as I grew older. I eventually met new people, built a purposeful career, bought a new car, found true love, and upgraded to a new doctor (who correctly diagnosed my disease—I wasn't going crazy!). However, it took time to find security and peace in adulthood.

My early twenties were unstable, and they caused me to wrestle with questions about my core identity. As a college student I battled with issues of self-worth, identity, and belonging. These insecurities were common in college, but I mistakenly thought that those problems would stay on campus when I graduated. It didn't cross my mind that adults still dealt with these issues. I'm embarrassed to admit it, but I was blindsided when my identity battle flared up again after graduation.

It turns out that identity struggles will challenge us in each new stage of life; there will always be fresh adversities that cause us to rethink how we see ourselves. My twenties were no exception to this rule, and I was forced to find answers to the same questions that I thought were put to rest in college: Who am I? What is my capacity in the workplace? Am I a leader? Am I lovable? Where do I belong?

Isolation and a lack of community were the common threads woven through all my emerging adult woes. I had moved to a new city for a new job. I was hours away from my college friends, family, and church community. I had no friends to help anchor my personal identity or to provide stability in my hardship.

These reflections might trigger similar memories from your own youth. Everyone struggles to some extent with building an identity in emerging adulthood, but not many people are prepared with a community to help them face the fight.

Emerging Adult Pain

Lonely identity formation is common among Millennials and Gen Zers alike. Our culture encourages them to live unbounded and free-flowing lives. They chase these cultural ideals only to miss out on the relational support that is so desperately needed. They find themselves in isolation—desperately craving community—but unaware of how to meaningfully bond themselves with others.

Take Samantha, for example. Samantha is currently twenty-three. Her friends describe her as a high achiever who is funny, personable, and outgoing. She's from middle America but was smart enough to get into a great school in New York City. It is hard to make friends in a new city, especially in NYC.

Sam has a great community back home but has struggled to connect with anyone in the big city. She hasn't been able to make any significant connections after trying to meet people at school, church, and the bars. Sam has a history of depression and anxiety. It's manifested at times in eating disorders, although that's been under control lately. But her anxiety still appears in the form of depression.

She feels so overwhelmed by schoolwork and city life that she can't seem to get out of bed on many mornings. Without any support system in the city, she has turned to the city nightlife as a way of self-medicating. Some days she feels great, but other days she experiences emotional drops. Her depression keeps her from functioning at the level that she knows she's capable.

Sam went to NYC to soar high in academy and career, but her emotional struggles have limited her studies to one class per semester. Her future has met a roadblock in depression and anxiety.

Sam is a classic case of emerging adult life. To some people she might sound like a fragile person, but she is experiencing the kind of insecurity that most in her age bracket feel. If you're under the age of thirty-five, then chances are good that you can connect with some aspects of Samantha's vulnerable experience. There are countless numbers of stories like hers, stories of people hurting through hardship. These tales make it obvious that the entry into adult life can be an entry into crisis.

Mental health statistics tell Samantha's story on a larger scale. The numbers reveal that something within these generations is going incredibly wrong. Clinical depression has recently increased for Gen Z by 63 percent.[1] And adults in the eighteen to twenty-five age range are now reporting more episodes of major depression than any other age bracket, including the elderly.[2]

Anxiety is also on the rise. One-fifth of adults suffer from anxiety but it's especially on the rise for young adults. College students are 50 percent more likely to feel overwhelmed than their parents were at the same age.[3] I recently visited a university in Tennessee where more than half of the freshmen self-reported serious struggles with anxiety.

Loneliness may be the source of these mental health issues. Gen Z reports as being the loneliest generation in America, taking the top spot from elderly who have traditionally held that title.[4] In truth, the whole of Western society feels the burden of loneliness. Only half of Americans have a meaningful conversation with someone else on an average day. Although the recent mental health crisis has affected every generation, it has been especially hard on young adults.[5]

Millennials and Gen Zers are increasingly antisocial, isolated, depressed, and anxious. These generations are experiencing a major mental breakdown that could define them for life. The question is: *Why?*

The Cultural Narrative: Journey Alone

We've empathized with the emerging adult experience. Now it's time to look under the hood at the cultural forces beneath it. This cultural narrative is one of the primary reasons we are experiencing generational breakdown on a mass scale.

The current cultural narrative reinforces the social trends that compel people into isolation. Emerging adults are sold a vision of life that requires them to live alone. They view themselves as living out a lonely journey of self-discovery. This narrative, the same one that drives the mental health crisis, also spurs on the big problem of the young adult church exodus.

The identity-making script is that a young adult must leave high school or college to discover who they truly are in contrast to their upbringing. They need to discover freedom from people, places, and traditions before they can find their true self. Identity cannot be given by anyone else; it must be discovered from within. Emerging adults graduate from high school or college with unlimited personal choices by which they are challenged to discover a new identity.

Luke Skywalker of the *Star Wars* film series is a classic example of how the cultural script influences people. Luke longed throughout his grade school years to leave his home planet, relationships, and family of origin to go discover who he truly was. Luke left for battle, unwilling to be defined by what he left behind.

Sam is another example. She left her hometown for the lights and allure of NYC. Most believe—whether they are able to articulate it or not—that unearthing an adult identity requires us to throw off the relationships and ties that defined us in childhood. Intimate companionship is a key to human happiness, but culture insists that we go on a lonely journey in early adulthood.

To understand how this ended up being the case, we must first understand our deepest cultural values and priorities. Only then can we grasp how the journey alone has become so appealing.

Freedom of choice has come to trump all other values for us. We believe that the greatest good in life is our ability to make whatever choices we want, and to be free to become whomever we desire.

The desire for increased personal freedom has become our society's unchallenged priority. Cultural critic and philosopher Charles Taylor refers to the plight of today's individual as "expressive individualism." This is "an understanding that each one of us has his/her own way of realizing our humanity, and that we are called to live that out (express it) rather than conform to models imposed by others (especially institutions)."[6]

Expressive individualism happens when personal identity is discovered within oneself and is expressed through personal action and consumer choice. Freedom of choice is so important because it gives us more options from which to express and build our personal identity.

We imagine building our own reality as a homeowner imagines designing a house. Each of us is a construction foreman who assembles a personal worldview and sense of identity from an endless list of options. Don't ask for help in this process. This building project is managed alone. How do we construct this house? We do this through the decisions we make as individuals.[7] We are in charge of expressing our own identity, and we do that through our choices and actions.

The Identity Foreman

Emerging adults are all identity foremen. Building a sense of self from the ground up preoccupies most young adults in your Christian community.

The identity foreman lives within his or her own construction of how the world works and builds a personal framework of truth. They resist help or assistance from anyone or anything else when it comes to making decisions that form their sense of who they are or how they should live.

Those who dare to borrow identity from family, faith, or upbringing are accused of being inauthentic because they did not construct their own identity apart from traditional values. For example, a person who practices their family's religion may be considered an inauthentic person for not experimenting with other religious options, or someone who doesn't move away from their hometown might be thought of as weak or unimaginative since they settled for a familiar place. They are forced to detach from any sense of belonging in their self-construction project. The identity foreman is radically individualistic and cannot use hand-me-down material to build a sense of self.

Authors Christian Smith and Patricia Snell wrote in their book *Souls in Transition*:

> They [Millennials] seem to presuppose that they are simply imprisoned in their own subjective selves, limited to their biased interpretations of their own sense perceptions, unable to know the real truth of anything beyond themselves.[8]

It is a daunting task to reject the places, people, and traditions that one grew up in, in hopes of developing an authentic self.[9] Emerging adults are yanked out of familiar high school or college settings and are forced to discover themselves in isolation. Uprooted from their deepest commitments, they are handed unlimited construction material—places to live, jobs to apply for, people to date—from which to build a new identity.

The major church exodus and mental health crisis should not be surprising to us! People are journeying alone and are carrying the enormous weight of identity-making. This work is dizzying and disorienting. It pits us against our deepest held convictions—including family, community, and religion. Our young adults are running a self-construction site with endless options. They are left alone—stripped of their blueprint—and are told to build a new identity.

The good news is this: God has uniquely positioned his church to heal lonely generations in our moment. The pages of Scripture and the power of the Holy Spirit can carry our beloved twenty-somethings into renewal. We only need look at the beginning pages of the Bible, and the life of the early church, to find the cure. God has given you the blueprint and the material needed to lead emerging adults through this process.

The church has a better story for Millennials and Gen Zers. God's narrative is a better one than the cultural narrative. Let's take a look at Scripture so you can rediscover God's blueprint for adult identity and community.

Created for Relationship

The best place to start is at the beginning, with Adam and Eve. God loved everything he created. He looked at the whole cosmos and said, "It is good." However, there was one exception to God's approval. God was disappointed when he saw Adam alone in isolation. In the Genesis creation story, God looked at Adam and said, "It is not good that the man should be alone" (Gen. 2:18a). God said this because humankind is created *for* relationship. Relationship itself has been, and always will be, at the core of human thriving. Scholar and theologian Josh McNall had this to say about the relational center of humankind: "As human beings, we were not only created *from* community (Father, Son, and Spirit), we were created *for* community. We were created to do life together—with God and with each other—so Adam gets a soul mate."[10]

Adam and Eve were created for one another. When Adam saw Eve he said, "This *at last* is bone of my bones and flesh of my flesh" (Gen. 2:23a, emphasis added). Adam waited to share his life with another person and was only satisfied when Eve appeared. Adam and Eve were more than made *for* each other. They were made *from* each other, and they shared life together. Each of us can understand Adam's longing to live life with others who are like us and who can understand us.

God himself is loving relationship (the Trinity). Humankind was created from the loving community of the Trinity, and we were intended to share in that life together. This is a fundamental and underlying reality of the God-created cosmos. The mystery of the Trinity reveals that relationship exists within the very person of God. He is three people who are unified in one (Father, Son, and Holy Spirit).

God is in a loving relationship with himself, and we are created in his image. He is our source of life and, in him, we see our most basic human need: intimate relationship. Our Creator beckons us first to know him intimately and to join the community of the Trinity.

Relationship is also at the heart of the story of Jesus. He came, lived a perfect life, died, and resurrected to break the powers of sin and death and to bring humankind back into relationship with God. Jesus instantaneously connects us to life-giving relationships through relationship with him. We automatically are joined into the community of the church when we come to know him.

The isolation of emerging adulthood saddens the heart of God. As Christians we know that we were never intended to live this way. It is counter to our basic beliefs about humanity and the very essence of the gospel. The cultural narrative of journeying alone violates the relational core of each person and has created a significant wound in the hearts of the average young adult.

The church has the good news. God has equipped us to meet these deep relational needs. Christian community is designed to be a unified body of believers who journeys the road of salvation and life together. God's healing prescription for lonely generations is written into the very DNA of the church.

The church could respond to the relational brokenness of emerging generations by providing forged families. *Forged families* are nonbiological families of people that bond together to overcome a common struggle. For our purposes, they are communities of interdependent young adults who bond together to follow Jesus through their twenties.

But let's be honest. There just aren't many Christian communities harnessing the power of real and raw family-like relationships. Some might attract young adults to a Sunday service or online experience, but a once-a-week experience isn't going to do the trick. Sunday attendance is not enough to form emerging adults in the light of their cultural narrative. What they need is a Christian family to live with from Monday to Saturday.

The leader that forges family throughout the week will make a difference in the lives of young believers. Any church can create space for authentic relationship. Do not be discouraged, or let your ministry die in the fight for emerging adult attendance. Forged families do not rely on the attendance of many, but on the bonds of a few. Any community of any size can be awakened to the renewal potential of forged families.

Rediscovering Relationships

Family-like community sits at the center of need for culture, emerging adulthood, and the church. We need not look any further than the book of Acts for a picture of what forged family looks like. Early Christian community was a place of belonging, commitment, and sacrifice. The Acts community ate together, worshipped together, shared their finances, and lived life as family.

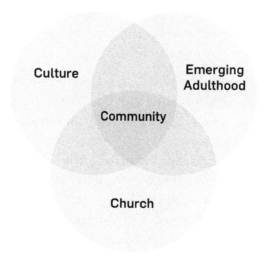

People did not walk out their salvation journey alone. New believers were immediately added to a community that was on the journey of salvation together. When the Holy Spirit fell on Pentecost (the birthday of the church), each person who responded became a member of God's family.[11]

These new believers weren't baptized into Sunday morning attendance, but into a family, a living body. The Holy Spirit appeared, convicted, saved, and brought together the family of God. New believers were immediately plunged into daily spiritual rhythms with other worshippers.

The classic passage Acts 2:42–47 (NIV) serves as a reminder of what community was like for the early church of believers:

> They devoted themselves to the apostles' teaching and to fellowship, to the breaking of bread and to prayer. Everyone was filled with awe at the many wonders and signs performed by the apostles. All the believers were together and had everything in common. They sold property and possessions to give to anyone who had need. Every day they continued to meet together in the temple courts. They broke bread in their homes and ate together with glad and sincere hearts, praising God and enjoying the favor of all the people. And the Lord added to their number daily those who were being saved.

Notice the intensity of this community. They lived with other believers and worshipped with them every day, both in the home and at the temple. This Christian family shared what they possessed and sacrificed for one another. Justice and mission happened as the natural overflow of their fellowship.

Acts 2 paints the picture of church as forged family. It was not enough for new disciples to live in isolation. They could not journey alone and be expected to survive in their faith. They needed to bond with other Jesus followers to be formed in his way.

It was family-like community that strengthened the church to mold people into Jesus' radical, countercultural image. The early apostles understood this and organized all the new disciples into household families.

I had the privilege of working at a campus ministry at a large state university for nearly a decade and have since networked with dozens of campus ministries across the country. Nearly every influential campus ministry—the ones that reach and form new Christians in emerging generations—shares one thing in common: an anointing for family-like community.

Ministries that provide space for emerging adults to center their campus life around shared teachings, discipleship, and worship impact those generations. The ministry I worked for at the University of Kentucky was not at all perfect. We had plenty of failures when it came to the community. Relationships are, after all, hard work. Regardless of the difficulty, most students would look back on that community and think of it as a source of healing, growth, and strength. They had daily options to pray together, worship, or to simply hang out.

The students in that ministry did more than attend events together. They mourned together, celebrated together, and ate together. It was a community where people were fully known. This outpost of kingdom life provided genuine friendship to a campus of strangers. It was a home away from home for hundreds of people who came to know Jesus through the community.

Friendships That Heal

We witnessed God heal college students from things like addiction, abortion wounds, and other deep emotional scars through shared intimacy in community.

Tristan is one emerging adult who received healing through community. He had two parents who battled PTSD and alcoholism throughout his youth. He dealt with the fallout of this difficulty in his college years and things got pretty nasty when he was a junior. There were multiple times that year when he pleaded with his father not to commit suicide and his mom experienced mental health issues because of the instability in the home. Tristan didn't live with his parents at the time, but he still felt the weight of those issues.

He was only able to cope with these trials because he had a true family-like community. He had this to say:

> I have a mom and a dad who both have PTSD, and had been relying heavily on alcohol over the past year, resulting in lots of fights and them not being emotionally present . . . This community has been my home away from home, a safe haven of sorts, and has helped me realize that, while my earthly parents may not always be there for me, my heavenly Father always will.

We are all tired of hearing the stories of deconstruction. The wall of identity-making can break anyone's faith and any church's community. However, you can transform stories of deconstruction into stories like Tristan's. What is needed is the strength of community.

Young adults need not journey through their twenties alone. Any Christian community can step in and help them forge a young adult family. These families are strong, enduring, and capable of making a real difference in Millennial/Gen Z lives. They are not easily worn away. The cultural tides cannot wash them out. They will not dissolve on a whim.

Family-like community will carry authentic religion in emerging generations. Forged families join in the muck of real life with one another, and leaders who build them will dig into the trenches alongside younger Christians. But be warned . . . family is messy. It's dirty. It's personal. It can happen in a church building, but it's better suited around the dining room table. Family cannot be programmed. It's organic, intimate, and requires vulnerability. Do not be intimidated by the dirty work that is required to create family-like relationships with emerging generations, but *do* count the cost. It will require your heart, your prayers, your spirit, and your resiliency. Those brave enough to act on the values of deep discipleship and intimate community will blaze the trail into the future of American Christianity. The question is: Will you be found alongside young adults on that venture?

The Wall of Distraction
Detoxing from Medi(a)cation

I got so bored that I started thinking about
existence! Do I matter? Do any of us? Is there a
master plan in the works? A grand design?
—Andy Dwyer, *Parks and Rec*

TECH ADDICTION HAS SHORTENED OUR ATTENTION
spans. Distracted minds have trouble focusing. Leaders are
constantly complaining about the absentmindedness of Gen Zers
and Millennials. They refuse to read books. They will not focus
during lectures and sermons. They must be entertained, or you
will lose their concentration. Emerging generations catch a lot of
flak for being mental zombies, but the truth is that most of our
attention spans have shortened over recent years.

And worse yet, distraction is having a real effect on our relationships. It does not matter if we are talking about the collapse of
community inside or outside of the church. Tech-addicted living
is one major reason why deep friendship is hard to come by for
today's young adults. Technology has thrown tiny blue-lit walls in
front of our faces that sidetrack us from the people we love.

You want to develop forged families, but the wall of distraction stands in the way of authentic community. No one wants to be

overlooked. Young adults especially want to be seen and known. They long to have their voices and their stories heard. And that's what forged families do. They tear down the wall of distraction to give their full attention to one another. They communicate love with eye contact, getting to know each other from the inside out.

There is nothing more attractive to young adults than communities of people who are simply present.

Can the emerging adults in your discipleship circles overcome the allure of the screen for the sake of seeing others? Can they unearth undistracted friendship? I believe they can. They can recover the art of meeting face-to-face with our help. And in doing so, they will see the goodness of God in one another. In this chapter, we will explore the wall of distraction and will see how a forged family can break through it.

Screens Pacify Teens

The van came to a screeching halt. We were lost in the Kenyan wilderness. The blazing hot sun beat down on us as we drove across the roadless plains. I looked out my window to see why we had pulled over—and there it was. Crouched in the grass next to our van was a wild cheetah! My heart sprung inside of me with excitement, but blood-pumping adrenaline quickly turned into tension. I was the designated cameraman for the trip and found myself in a dilemma. Do I fumble around for the camera? Or do I take in the sight of this cheetah, and commit it to memory? It was the spring of 2004 and camera phones weren't a thing yet.

I was the only person who had the option to capture this moment on film. If I didn't pull out the camcorder, then no one else would. I had a split second to make my decision . . . I let the film bag sit on the floor of the van.

The cheetah was too spectacular and too graceful for me to ruin the moment by fumbling around for a camera. So I simply watched what came next. The cheetah sat for a few seconds. She looked up at us and casually stood to her feet. Then she slinked away in the direction of the orange African sun.

I quickly realized that I had made the right choice. I would have missed those precious few serendipitous seconds if I had rummaged around to look for my camera. I didn't know it then, but that kind of split-second choice would be a decision I would have to make thousands of times in the coming decades.

This screen game is played multiple times every day. We may not feel like we miss something as glorious as a wild cheetah, but we make the same type of decision constantly. We are continuously asked the question: "Do I live in the moment or do I grab a device?" This question lingers over us during face-to-face conversations, meetings, church events, and class. It feels like there is always a buzzing phone we could grab, a TV on the wall to watch, or a picture that we could take. There are dozens of ways that we are tempted to leave the present world and escape into the digital realm of technology.

We have been trained to leave our physical world and hone into the connected online space. Gen Z is the first generation in human history to live in a fully connected world from birth. A distracted existence is the only one they know.

Gen Z is the first generation in human history that's had to fight intensely for in-person interaction. They grew up fighting for their parent's attention. *Listen to me with your whole face* was their heart-cry while growing up.

And while technology took away their parents' attention, it was also given to them as a reward. Parents used screens to pacify their teens. Tech was treated as a way to make Gen Z happy, distracted, or relaxed.

These tiny technological squares trained them from an early age to trade in real-world moments for flashing lights on a screen. In truth, technology has trained all of us, regardless of our age bracket. The tech industry knows how to hook us on our devices.

Fluorescent lights and fun noises reduce our willpower to that of monkeys in a cage. Technology serves practical purposes in our lives, but we don't go to them because they're practical. We go to our devices because they make us feel good. Think about it—do you more often get on your phone for practical reasons or for fun?

Our devices operate like theme parks. You enter for the bright lights and rides, but then you smell the funnel cakes, and then follow the games further in. One thing leads to another, and you're in the center of the park without ever having realized you left the entrance. This is how distraction works with our tech devices. The sights and sounds on our phones, computers, and tablets are designed to entice us.

Our brains receive dopamine when our phones ring. We receive a literal physical feeling of satisfaction when we hear the blip and feel the buzz in our pockets.[1] We are mindlessly sucked in by the fun sights and sounds and find it difficult to leave once we're pulled inside. Author J. Ellsworth Kalas wrote:

> You and I live in a time when distraction has taken on a life of its own. Its powers have become so sophisticated that much of the time we don't even realize it is at work in us and on us. Some of the most creative and imaginative minds in our culture have a full-time assignment to get our attention and to move it away from other matters.[2]

It can be hard to put down a device once we've picked it up. These machines are designed to keep us engaged. Devices and apps work like the funnel cakes and games at an amusement park to keep us using the device once we've begun. Endless click trails and binge-watching are the norm for device junkies. We go to our phones or laptops for one thing (often useful things) and before we know it, we've spent a half hour scrolling and watching aimlessly.

Your time and distraction are money in someone else's pocket. The more you scroll, the more ads you can see. The more ads you see, the more money goes into the pockets of marketers, app designers, and tech companies. Every day you are being lured into a black hole of distraction by design.

Distraction Shapes Us

We at first attach ourselves to tech devices because they serve a practical purpose for us. GPS on our phones help us navigate the roads. Fandango helps us buy movie tickets before they're sold out. Tinder helps us . . . ahem . . . you get the point. We adopt new technology because it benefits our lives, but in the end, our tech may manipulate us and our world more than we control it.[3] Author Patrick Deenan wrote: "What is supposed to allow us to transform our world is instead transforming us, making us into creatures to which many, if not most of us, have not given our 'consent.'"[4]

We have granted the devices in our pockets, in our homes, and on our screens a unique power that wasn't consciously handed over. They have the power to shape the way we relate to ourselves, to God, and to others. We have fallen into new rhythms and patterns of life that we never originally intended. We currently find ourselves in a distraction battle with our devices and, as we've discussed before, relationships and community are central to human flourishing. Intimacy with God and other people is the core reason we were created, but we are unconsciously being shaped to live lives distracted from one another. *Our relational health is at stake and, ultimately, so is our humanity.*

People are becoming increasingly more aware of how distracted we truly are. There is a growing concern that tech addiction is outside of anyone's control. The cultural conversation has reached the point to where Apple started sending weekly iPhone screen-time updates.

People were shocked at how long they were spending on their phone every day. I talked to young adults who were appalled to find out they were spending five, six, and even seven hours daily on their devices. Younger generations are being negatively impacted by device overuse—aren't we all?—and an adequate solution has not yet been suggested.

The statistics on Gen Z screen time and device use help to illustrate where we've come to in relation to our devices. Research done by Jean M. Twenge shows how this generation was taken over by screen distraction in high school. Her studies display the relational effects that phone screen time has had across a generation. She found that the average Gen Z high school senior spent six hours a day looking at screens.[5] Screen usage spiked and along with it came a decline of time with friends. The number of teens who spend time with friends daily has dropped by 50 percent in the last fifteen years. She found that screen time within that age group is connected to higher depression rates and higher levels of unhappiness.[6]

The groups of students who made up these surveys are currently emerging adults. They know firsthand the effects that screen use has had on themselves and their relationships. What was true for them, then, is true for the rest of us. Screen time is on the rise and our emotional well-being and relationships are suffering as a result.

Medi(a)cation

Device distraction is a way that we have trained ourselves to avoid awkward interactions with God and each other. We mindlessly engross ourselves in them while the earth keeps spinning and evolving. The distracted person remains stationary, and the living world moves along.

Devices take the grand landscape of life and shrink it into a tiny rectangle. What once caused awe, inspiration, and creativity now bores us. We turn to our devices instead, as a way to medicate our casual discomfort.

We have willfully surrendered our alone time and the ability to appreciate nature along with it. We live in a world with awe-inspiring scope, but it goes unnoticed by most of us. Tech distraction is the latest step in a centuries-long process of stripping our sense of God and awe from the world around us.

Western society was once obsessed with the mystery of the cosmos, but since the Enlightenment (rise of the scientific and naturalist worldview), we have dissected the natural world and removed God from our collective belief set. We have discredited any experience outside of a quantifiable event as imaginary. God's existence is largely denied by scientific culture and the grand mysteries of the cosmos have collapsed into the enclosed and measurable natural world around us.

The Enlightenment was a massive step in shrinking our sense of purpose and well-being in the cosmos because it removed the expectation that each person will experience the mystery of God within it. Ronald Rohlheiser wrote: "If there is no God, we are pathetically abandoned, and robbed of deep meaning, final significance, and the ultimate loving graciousness which alone vindicates love and makes life worth living."[7]

Technology has further stripped a sense of God's presence from our collective imagination. Our world, our sense of mystery, awe, and wonder has shrunk yet again. Technology occupies our brains in a way that halts our imaginations and robs us of the freedom to experience a potentially breathtaking world.

The world has lost its divine purpose and society has a problem with meaninglessness as a result. We escape emotions of emptiness and dread by fixating on our devices. They have become our protection against the pain of purposelessness. Motivational speaker and author Brené Brown wrote: "Disengagement is the issue underlying the majority of problems I see in families, schools, communities, and organizations and it takes many forms . . . We disengage to protect ourselves from vulnerability, shame, and feeling lost and without purpose."[8]

The question is: Could our feelings of purposelessness be a sign that God is pressing in on us? Transcendent longing could be our sign that he actually exists. It beckons and calls us to recognize God himself. C. S. Lewis believed these desires to be signs that point toward a spiritual reality: "If I find in myself a desire which no experience in this world can satisfy, the most probable explanation is that I was made for another world."[9]

Our transcendent longings are meant to lead us to thoughts of God and, perhaps, to a discovery of meaning. But these discomforting thoughts now lead us to our phones. We self-medicate our personal feelings and spiritual problems by going to our devices.

Many disengage from the world as means of coping. Screens are used to pacify the transcendent urges that are designed to guide us into God's presence. Andy Crouch, in his book *The Tech-Wise Family*, wrote:

> So here is one result of our technology: we become people who desperately need entertainment and distraction because we have lost the world of meadows and meteors. Quite literally lost—where can my own children go to see a meadow? How far from the city would we have to drive for them to see a meteor in the night sky? But very nearby are technological forms of distraction, from video games to constantly updated social media. They do little to develop our abilities to wait, pay attention, contemplate, and explore—all needed to discover the abundance of the ordinary.[10]

My writing desk overlooks an urban park. This park is an oasis of natural life in the middle of the city. Students come to the only spot for miles around where they can experience the natural world but, unfortunately, most of them walk their dogs with their phones in front of their faces. I watch person after person walk past marvelous trees and step over large natural stones, all while staring at their phones.

Our intimacy with God is harmed when there isn't mental space left for him to occupy. Kalas wrote: "Distraction instead keeps faith at the margins of life. And if there is anything that Christianity cannot abide, it is marginality."[11]

Distracted Friendship

God is not the only person that we're tempted to ignore by looking at our devices. Can you remember a time when you have set down your phone, only to discover that someone is looking deadpan at you, waiting to continue a conversation? That is an embarrassing moment, but is one that happens to each of us from time to time. It is tempting to abandon in-person conversations for a quick look at our phone (or a TV or tablet).

Sherry Turkle said that in these moments each of us is "pause-able."[12] Face-to-face interaction is hurt by our constant tech use. Phones in our pockets or on the table cause us to mentally multi-task while having face-to-face conversation. We struggle to listen to the person in front of us while also being conscious of the rectangle in our pocket. It is difficult to be present with the face-to-face while simultaneously being connected to people digitally.

Our devices connect us to too many people and streams of communication at once. They provide seamless connection to the world and provide endless opportunity for distraction. We trade in meaningful face-to-face moments for dozens of irrelevant interactions. They are distractions that we can't escape so long as a device is near us.

Distraction competes with the presence of others. The most meaningful conversations happen when two people are fully engaged with one another. Intimacy happens when we bring all of ourselves to the moment with another person.

Think of the deep conversations you have had in your life . . . conversations about friends and family, death and marriage, faith and love. They involve qualities such as trust, confidentiality, safety, and patience. These traits are each hindered by phone use during a conversation.

We break trust when we choose to pause a conversation to take a call or a text. We break confidentiality when we send signals to a friend that, "Your life isn't important enough for me to hold off on communicating with others." How many intimate moments have been ruined because someone wants to throw the perfect moment up on an Instagram story? Significant memories like birthday parties, weddings, and deep conversations are halted when we reach for our phones and pause real life for a camera.

We develop weighty friendships through face-to-face interactions. It shouldn't surprise us that, statistically speaking, Gen Zers spends less time with friends if their screen time increases. It also shouldn't be a surprise that depression also follows the same correlation.

In-person relationships are humanizing. They help us feel alive and have the power to restore a person whose spirit is dwindling. Emerging generations ache for friends with whom they can smile, laugh, and dance—friends who are physically present.

You can provide spaces for thriving friendship within your Christian community. The church can restore vintage human relationships. However, we will lose the potent power of forged families if our communities are built around distracted friendships.

Hosting young adults in disturbance-free environments is a good way to enhance forged families. But you must first teach, model, and value presence. Communities will be present with each other only when they are made up of present people. Undistracted lives pave the way for present community.

Solitude Connects Us

The practice of solitude is monumental for developing an undistracted life. Solitude forces us to confront the emotions that are so easily stuffed by device distraction.

Let's look to "philosopher" Andy Dwyer for a good example of solitude. This absentminded and beloved character on the sitcom *Parks and Rec* begins a job as a security guard in one episode. He spends time alone while patrolling an abandoned government building. The pressure of being alone with his thoughts builds and, after twenty minutes, he calls for help. In a manic state he says, "I got so bored that I started thinking about existence! Do I matter? Do any of us? Is there a master plan in the works? A grand design?"[13]

Goofy example, I know. But these are truly the types of healthy questions that rise to the surface when we spend time alone. Alan Noble wrote: "The constant distraction of our culture shields us from the kind of deep, honest reflection needed to ask why we exist and what is true."[14]

We will never be emotionally or spiritual whole without confronting the great and small questions of life. Maturity will remain beyond our grasp if we never muster up the courage to confront the thoughts that arise when we're alone.

Device medi(a)cation keep us from knowing ourselves and God. Andy's breakdown on *Parks and Rec* made me laugh, but it also highlights the need for a practice of solitude.

The first step toward equipping young adults with a lifestyle of solitude is to model it ourselves. It is up to each one of us to embrace the tension of being alone without distraction. Only then can we become whole people and be able to contribute to meaningful relationships. True and undistracted solitude is the

Christian response to the wall of device distraction that isolates us. Solitude is the practice of intentional and healthy disengagement from distraction and from others. Ruth Haley Barton, in her book *Sacred Rhythms,* wrote:

> Solitude is a place. It is a place in time that is set apart for God and God alone, a time when we unplug and withdraw from the noise of interpersonal interactions, from the noise, busyness and constant stimulation associated with life in the company of others. . . . Most important, solitude is a place inside myself where God's Spirit and my spirit dwell together in union.[15]

God will shape us when we spend undistracted time alone in his presence.

We cannot control the presence of God, but we can control the rhythms of our lives. Our rhythms shape us. We are unlikely to be molded by the presence of God if we don't put ourselves in positions to encounter that presence.

Living a life of device distraction will discourage the experience of God's presence and keep us disconnected and emotionally discouraged. Conversely, God can shape us into relationally connected and emotionally whole people when we choose solitude.

Solitude gives God space to lead us in Scripture and heal us in prayer. Our lives—and the souls of emerging adults—can heal when we give God space to speak to us about our questions, doubts, insecurities, and emotions.

Peace in solitude allows us to have peace in community.

Theologian Dietrich Bonhoeffer didn't mince words when he said, "Let him who cannot be alone beware of community. It will only do harm to himself and to the community."[16] I wonder if Bonhoeffer were alive today if he would say, "Let him who cannot be alone and undistracted beware of community." We need to have wholeness in God—and in solitude—before we can meaningfully love others.

Emotionally and spiritually healthy people are capable of truly loving others. Solitude allows us to become a safe place for other people to experience intimate relationships because we are satisfied with God and no longer need to self-medicate with distraction.

Distracted and anxious people make for shallow communities, but emerging adults who master the art of solitude will be a gift to others. They can offer their friends a present attentiveness, a listening ear, and a caring heart. Henri Nouwen wrote: "Solitude does not pull us away from our fellow human beings but instead makes real fellowship possible."[17]

Undistracted Friendship

The art of presence starts with solitude and extends into our everyday relationships. We can help protect the sacredness of human connection by cultivating communities in distraction-free environments. Think about the dynamics of the room where you gather young adults. Can they see each other? Do they ever face one another or are they always facing a presenter? Is the meeting space simple, or does is blaze with bright lights and large screens?

It is impossible to imagine a distracted Jesus in Scripture. Think about Jesus with the woman at the well. What if he asked her to pause her adultery confession so he could respond to a quick text? Or imagine one of the disciples zoning out during the Last Supper to watch a TV on the wall in the Upper Room. These pictures are hilarious to think about, but they are the realities of our common gathering spaces. How many sacred moments are wasted because our communities meet in distraction-prone environments?

You can protect the sacredness of spiritual friendship by forging families in simple spaces. Bring people together in clean rooms where they can be present with God and with one another. Allow for genuine relationships to break through the awkwardness of silence. Encourage eye contact. Listen to people with your whole face.

You will help emerging adults to bond tightly with Christian community through the practice of solitude and environments of presence. They will not only find that they love the presence of God, but that they have friends in the faith as well. These relationships will dive below the surface of shallow interaction.

No one remains a stranger in forged families. They will be present to understand one another's stories, experiences, and hearts. A deep soul resonance and trusted unity will develop as they discover how much they have in common. Intimacy, love, and humanity can be restored to their relationships with a little intentionality.

Twenty-somethings are desperate to be known from the inside out. Tear down the wall of distraction, and you are likely to forge an authentic and attractive emerging adult family.

CHAPTER THREE

The Wall of Competition
Competing in the Social Media Arena

If you ain't first, you're last.
—Ricky Bobby, *Talladega Nights*

CHURCHES ARE NOT THE ONLY LOCAL ORGANIZATIONS that have fallen by the wayside in recent years. Much has been made about the deterioration of grassroots-level civil institutions. Nearly every form of association has seen a decrease and drop-off in involvement.

Neighborhood coalitions, churches, clubs, and societies were once the places where people went to share their opinions and get to know one another. We would argue, debate, and eventually rally together around common goals, dreams, and desires. These once necessary collaborative public spaces are vanishing. Their disappearance is happening in correlation with the rise of social media interaction.

You have surely seen the impact of this in your church leadership. Maybe your church has divided after a frivolous argument on Facebook. Or maybe people in your community have stopped talking to one another because of a disagreement on Twitter. Or perhaps you have been personally attacked because of an opinion shared online.

Committed community seems to be rapidly deteriorating within our society. People have left grassroots institutions to retreat into their homes, trading in-person relationships for social media interaction in the process.

Emerging generations are experiencing similar relational effects. They have major problems embracing real and raw community because of the artificial friendships that are peddled to them online.

This chapter will show us how young adults struggle to build community in light of social media competition and comparison. It is a uniquely strong problem for their age group, one that blocks them from authentic community within the church and with one another. We can break through that barrier by taking a closer look at what is causing it.

Gen Z especially faces a whole host of community problems, being the first generation to grow up on social media. They have substituted real and raw relationships for the digital world of influencers and ads. They have learned how to avoid being truly known by projecting a curated image of themselves online.

We have already discussed the identity problems that young adults experience. They are identity foremen who construct their self-image from the ground up. Social media adds to the confusion of that process. They are able to project multiple identities on multiple platforms and can choose to be an entirely different person online than in physical life.

Not to mention the fact that false online facades keep them from truly knowing each another. They are social chameleons, having learned how to wear a different mask for each friend group and situation. The self-image that they share online can change on a dime to meet the needs of the moment.

Social media–driven relationships are layered with competition and comparison. Emerging generations now socialize in a superficial digital space that breeds jealousy and fosters little true transparency. Connections are flimsy. Friendships are easily broken. It is easier for them to flee a friend than to work through conflict.

The fluidity of online relationships makes it hard for the church to bond with these generations and for these generations to bond with one another. We want to see twenty-somethings brought together in a common love for Jesus. This will require that our communities live alongside one another not just online, but in physical transparency. Forged families are made up of authentic relationships that break through the wall of comparison that is driven by online interactions.

Genuine discipleship communities tear through the barrier of superficial comparison. The people within them fight to get to know one another as their true selves. They love each other for the person underneath the facade.

And can I be honest for just one second about why I think the forged family strategy is such good news? I want to pull back the curtain to share my insecurity around the social media space. I'm just not good at building an online presence. I'm no marketing mind or a design genius. Famous people are not going to mention me on Instagram. My content is unlikely to go viral. Some people have a knack for establishing an online social presence, and I am not one of them. I feel behind the curve.

It is important for you to realize that you can impact emerging generations with or without hyper-engaging online profiles. You do not need thousands of followers to tear down the wall of competition. Young adults are hungry for real relationships that break out beyond the social media world. Every one of us can help them do that.

The road to church renewal is found off the grid. Leaders who form tight-knit communities of emerging adults will ditch the online identity game for a genuinely authentic form of in-person relationship. Forged families are transparent, vulnerable, and deeply personal. For them, commitment overrides competition.

If You Ain't First, You're Last!

"If you ain't first, you're last!" Ricky Bobby lives by this life code in the movie *Talladega Nights*. Rejected by his father as a child, Ricky uses this phrase to fuel his NASCAR career and to prove himself to his father. Coming in second isn't an option for Ricky Bobby. This funny catchphrase sticks with a person long after they watch the movie. It's funny, not just because it is an insane code to live by, but also because some people are actually tempted to live by it.

Everyone knows someone who has adopted this life philosophy. For them, coming in second in anything is the end of the world. This competitive spirit might show up in sports, board games, classrooms, or social media. (For me, it's basketball.) We live in a society built off the merit of winning.

Competition is an everyday reality, and some people just can't turn off their need to be superior to the rest of us. Coming in second place is a huge blow to some people's ego and losing is tough to handle emotionally. Some of us live by the Ricky Bobby axiom, whether we know it or not.

Society signals to us that we should view each other as competitors. We size each other up in every sphere of life. This starts at a young age. Students are ranked based on athleticism, smarts, and popularity. It is inbred in us that winning against others is the goal of life.

Not only do students have to deal with all of the classic competitive spaces, but they now have to deal with the social media popularity game. The pressure has been on Gen Zers from a young age to produce "likes" online. Their timelines are full of peers trying to look as good and impressive as possible. The temptation is to join in on the popularity game by curating the perfect online persona in order to keep up appearances.

Think about the cultural shift that has taken place over the last twenty years. Older generations were once worried about keeping up with the Joneses. The Joneses, in this hypothetical scenario, were the anonymous neighbor family who had everything together and made our parents jealous. That seems like *Leave It to Beaver*–type history now.

Today's emerging adults feel pressure to keep up with the Joneses, the Kardashians, and every other Instagram influencer. They are constantly bombarded with images of other people living their best lives. Even I don't go a day without my high school and college friends bragging about their advances and promotions online.

People post every time they buy a new car or house, get married, have children, or graduate from a program. We are meant to celebrate with them, but even the strongest people can get trapped in cycles of jealousy. Social media taps into our insecurities and can put us at odds with the people we know.

Hyperconnected but Relationally Starved

Emerging generations know that social media companies cannot provide the relationships they promise. Social media executives act a little bit like the park owner from *Jurassic Park*. The careless old man was happy to clone dinosaurs and make a profit, but when the raptors started eating people, he had a tough time admitting there were downsides to his science. Social media companies have given us a model for human connection in the digital age, but their model does not effectively replace in-person relationships.

Sure, social websites streamline connection, making communication easier than ever before. But we are suffering from relationship quantity over quality. It is all too obvious that our emotional needs are not met from constant communication but, rather, from quality of friendship. A long in-person conversation feels like a relational T-bone steak, while a quick meme or GIF from a friend is more like a fun-sized candy bar. The former meal will grow and sustain you. And while the latter meal is fun, eating it will keep you malnourished.

Research shows that internet communities have emotional downsides for twenty-somethings. Facebook is the most widely used social media service, so they have received the majority of the studies. They show that Facebook causes people to experience stress,[1] and some have found Facebook to be directly linked to unhappiness.[2]

These statistics make sense when you think about it. When was the last time you browsed Instagram or Facebook and left feeling better about your own life? We rabidly consume social media in hopes of staying connected, but often feel sour when logging off. We are promised relationships and are delivered discontentment.

This is a major downside to social media, but we're addicted to it and most of us can't stop using it. Seventy-two percent of American adults engage in some form of social media.[3] Facebook is the most popular online social platform and the average adult Facebook member uses it more than fifty minutes a day![4] It's no secret that social media harms us. Yet, we are social media junkies. Many of us are so addicted to social media that we won't even attempt to leave the platform.[5] Social media exposes our insecurities and, yet, we consume it mindlessly. Richard Plass and James Cofield wrote in their book, *The Relational Soul*: "When we are preoccupied with maintaining an image that the soul was not created to maintain, we grow emotionally weary. We become disillusioned and discouraged without knowing why. God feels distant and so do others. The closeness we desperately need and want eludes us."[6]

Arena of Competition

Meditating on pictures and videos of other people living their best lives is a recipe for feeling down about your own reality. I don't know about you, but I have to guard myself against negativity while viewing other people's accounts. I cannot view other pastors' social profiles while in a bad mood. I'll size myself and my ministry up against their accounts. This inevitably ends in me judging them or feeling jealous. Neither of those are good outcomes! That's the danger of online relationships. Social media platforms are arenas of competition where our lives are put on display and judged in contrast with others.

The irony is that social media does not represent our true selves. Posts are carefully selected, meticulously edited, and presented at just the right time. People curate the image they want to send, rarely representing the true state of their lives. We are guilty of projecting falsified lives with fake images.

Pictures are doctored and manipulated to make us look more appealing. This is especially true for emerging generations. A recent study out of the City University of London shows that 90 percent of young women use filters to change their physical features before posting a picture online.[7]

What drives young women to spend time editing their online pictures before posting? Comparison. Shame. Competition. Perfection. Fear. These feelings drive our online interactions, but they should have no place within forged families.

Rabbi Jonathan Sacks put it like this in his book *Morality*:

Comparing ourselves with others is one of the most deeply rooted of all human instincts, but the terms of the comparison change when we find ourselves measuring the reality of our own lives against the edited, sometimes artificially enhanced versions of other lives that we encounter on social media. One of the most striking new phenomena is FOMO (Fear of Missing Out). . . . In the past, if your friends were invited to a party to which you were not, this may have given you some anxiety, but at least it wasn't public. Today, everything is public. Everything is shared. Everything is there for a presentation of the self, and the

selfie. Social media invites us into a world of "advertise-
ments for myself" and a competition for attention that
few can win.[8]

Social media can foster more *rejection* than *connection*. The
arena of competition keeps us divided and in shame.

Influencers are good at capitalizing on the insecurities gener-
ated through social app comparison. Self-help gurus are popular.
Self-care and self-improvement are also booming industries for
influencers to tap in to. These accounts range from anything
like online fitness coaches to nutritionists to pseudo-religious
sages. Millions follow their profiles to feel better about their own
lives and to find direction. According to an article in the *New
York Times*: "The whole economy of Instagram is based on our
thinking about our selves, posting about our selves, working
on our selves."[9]

Social media creates the competition problem and *then* sells
solutions. There are plenty of online options to choose from for
self-improvement. Popular YouTube stars have thousands of
followers commit to extreme health challenges, diets, and self-
betterment programs. Master classes and life coaches are a dime
a dozen. People feel comparison shame, and in the same instant,
are sold the idea of a better self.

Comparison is a sickness that makes vulnerability in friendship nearly impossible.

The Shift from Network to Media

The superficiality of social media creates a barrier between
emerging generations and the church. Our natural instinct is to
reach them by creating as alluring a digital presence as possible.
Maybe we can make a difference with Gen Zers and Millennials
by winning the online popularity game.

This is a natural thought to buy into. The problem with it is that young adults (Gen Zers, especially) are quick to sniff out social media sales jobs. An online campaign of glitz and glam signals to them that a community is inauthentic, unlikely to be truly concerned with their best interests. They are all too used to being sold experiences online. They want their faith communities to lead them with a different set of values.

The online space has not always felt exploitative. Facebook and Myspace were first referred to as *social networks*. Networks are intended to connect and build relationships. But the reality of the space has been revealed in the title change. Over the years online sharing platforms evolved from networking to media. *Social media* is the result of a marketing revolution of digital relationships. The change in language is subtle, but it's profoundly true. Social apps are now media hubs where we go to sell ourselves to others and to buy into certain kinds of lifestyles.

Young adults are all too aware that social media is a new marketplace, where they are sold an idealized version of life. Ads have even taken over personal accounts. Online sales campaigns leave younger generations feeling gross and manipulated. They are always being sold something and realize that digital marketers overpromise and underdeliver. We want to protect our Christian communities from leaving this online impression.

Fyre, the Story of Capitalism Comparison

You need look no further than the Fyre Festival for an example as to why Gen Z is so disgusted by social marketing campaigns. The Fyre Festival had a brilliant promotional strategy. Months before the festival, its organizers threw a party with famous rappers and models on a private island. The star-studded cast enjoyed booze, yachts, and music on the Caribbean Sea. Photo and video captured the raucous scene and was paired with information about the upcoming festival, and the images hit social media with force. Fyre Festival organizers paid influencers to post the promotional content and the event became an instant online phenomenon. The marketing campaign had all the glitz, glam, and sex appeal that the internet could handle.

Event organizers sold hundreds of thousands, if not millions, of dollars' worth of tickets to the festival, months in advance. They did this without having a single band signed, room reserved, or food vendor booked. People bought tickets for the event they saw promoted online but it was a total sham. Fans arrived at the advertised island at the time the music festival was promoted but there were no musical acts, food, or lodging.

Marketers sold a fake music festival by giving people a picture of the life they wish they could be living. They captured people's attention by posting a private island beach party with models. The pictures and videos were too seductive for many gullible emerging adults to pass up.

Our economy (just like social media) is centered on selling us a picture of the good life.

Marketers want to capture the heart of the youth. They show us a compelling life, the life we should supposedly be living, and then try to sell us that life. The Fyre Festival promo didn't represent reality. The lifestyle shoot was fake and did not represent what was actually being sold. The images were used to attract desperate people with an idealized vision of life.

The festival flopped because it oversold a lifestyle and an event that it couldn't produce. This is classic marketing. It convinces us that we are one product, trip, or consumer choice away from having the life we want. Mark Sayers wrote: "A consumer order as exists in our world is powered by our constant dissatisfaction. To foster a sense of dissatisfaction, the world must offer us everything, and the beautiful world does indeed seem to promise such a feat."[10]

The Fyre Festival capitalized on people's FOMO by convincing them that they could live an elite lifestyle for a weekend. This is the kind of sales job that emerging generations are used to encountering on their social media.

Social media has even commercialized friendship. The number-one place we go to manage our relationships has become a marketplace of people where we try to sell ourselves and our lives for views, likes, comments, and prestige. Social media encourages us to mine our relationships for likes. Some even go as far as to try and monetize their friendships by pushing personal brands and pyramid scheme products, hoping to turn their friendship influence into actual monetary gain.

Young adults use their accounts to sell products and to brand themselves to their friends. They look to monetize the digital space and attempt to use their relationship circles as a way to make money. Personal accounts peddle things like essential oils, boutique gifts, and workout programs. Social websites turn friends into potential clients and change the dynamics of once pure relationships.

Twenty-somethings are constantly being sold to by everyone online: businesses, friends, and even churches. That is why we must be careful with how we portray our faith communities digitally. You will make emerging generations feel exploited if you promote in the wrong way. The church can easily avoid this by choosing a different tool to break through the wall of competition.

The Radical Act of Listening

I sat down with a college freshman who recently baptized five friends into the church. I asked him how he shares Jesus. He said, "I invite my classmates to coffee. They share their story. I listen. I ask lots of questions and show real interest. I let them know that Jesus cares too."

This wonderful college freshman is leading all of us into church renewal. He has cracked the code for reaching emerging generations. The secret sauce is this: creating space to be known. He listens, values, cherishes, and celebrates each person. This communicates love to his generation.

Listening is a radical act, especially when compared to all the online social dynamics that we've talked about in this chapter. Young adult social media has become a space for comparison. It is an arena of competition where emerging generations are made to feel insecure and unworthy. Marketers exploit their desire for human connection as a means to sell products.

What if your forged family modeled a different path for relationship? What if you were able to gather twenty-somethings around restorative values for friendship? Imagine creating a community where there was genuine interest in others; where people were free from sales jobs and comparison; and people asked what they could give, not what they could take.

Communities of renewal do just that. They value knowing people from the inside out and are comprised of individuals who want to give of themselves without taking from others. This posture breaks below the surface level of identity.

People want to be known beyond the projected online self. Forged families that create space for transparency and vulnerability will gain the trust of these skeptical generations. Communities that show genuine interest in one another are an absolute oasis for those stuck in the online relational desert. If you (and your forged family) open a listening ear, then you will win the day with young adults.

Listening communities will be communities of integrity. The Latin root for *integ* means "completeness" or "whole." Having *integrity* means re-*integrating* each part of the self into a complete whole. Young adult personalities are fractured along many different social media profiles and friend groups. The images they create of themselves are false, and some have lost the ability to know who they truly are. However, people who are truly known can discover who they truly are.

Intimate relationships help young adults integrate all their images and projections into a whole and complete person.[11] Online facades will wash away with a listening ear, and a complete person will emerge. Others-interested communities heal young Christians and see them become emotionally and spiritually whole people. Forged families are communities of integrity.

Celebration

I joined a campus ministry staff when I finished undergrad. I stepped into a new job, on a new campus, with a new group of people who did not know me. It was intimidating. I was on pins and needles as to whether I would be accepted. There was one thing that broke through my insecurity and hesitation: celebration.

Celebration is kryptonite to competition. Fear of rejection wastes away when you are recognized for your positive qualities. I know this from experience. People at the campus ministry quickly learned my name and bestowed an endearing nickname to me. Some on staff wrote me personalized handwritten notes for encouragement. There were even moments of spontaneous applause when I did something well.

That campus community had a built-in culture of celebration. I was not special and was not the only person who received gifts, letters, and spontaneous applause. Those happened on regular occasions. Staff took time to laugh with and encourage new people. They set an environment of joy.

I love that Scripture refers to the kingdom of God as a matter of *righteousness, joy, and peace in the Holy Spirit* (Rom. 14:17). Any forged family, a Spirit-filled community, will be countercultural in its joy and celebration. According to Dallas Willard:

> Celebration is the completion of worship, for it dwells on the greatness of God as shown in his goodness to our world, in conjunction with our faith and confidence in God's greatness, beauty, and goodness. We concentrate on our life and world as God's work and as God's gift to us. Typically this means that we come together with others who know God to eat and drink, to sing and dance, and to relate stories of God's action for our lives and our people.[12]

You can shine through the morose relational atmosphere that emerging adults exist in by doing things like throwing parties! Or feast in honor of people within your community. Buy gifts for birthdays. Write notes for each other. Have times of encouragement where you set aside time to call out the good you see in one another.

Where will young adults be celebrated, if not within the church? What could possibly be more attractive than communities that take time to stop and savor the goodness of life?

As a leader, you can set a culture of celebration for your forged family. Laugher and love will break through the wall of competition. Young adults won't feel exploited, but safe; not marketed to, but served; not compared, but cherished. Emerging generations will come to life in your community if they are seen, known, and encouraged.

CHAPTER FOUR

The Wall of Self-Sufficiency
Bridging the Gap between Your Capacity and Calling

*May a broken God be known in the earth beneath
our feet. May our souls behold humility.*
—Will Reagan, *Looking for a Savior*

YOUNG ADULTS DON'T HATE CHRISTIANITY. GEN ZERS and Millennials are not inherently anti-religion. Atheism is not why Gen Zers and Millennials are leaving the faith in droves. Our big problem of the emerging adult exodus is not caused by intense church opposition.

The issue is that twenty-somethings don't see a practical need for church. They are altogether indifferent toward religion. Apathy is one key reason that many of our communities are missing this age group.

They have a lot going on. Their lives are busy. Their stage of life demands a lot from them and it's hard to see how life with God would make a difference. They are consumed with the practical needs of adulthood and find Christian community to be . . . inessential.

Young adults wear blinders. Financial and career success is their sole focus. The weight of becoming self-sufficient is

49

all-consuming. The struggle to become a stable adult eats up all of their time and focus and leaves little room for friendship or the church.

The wall of distraction and the wall of competition are recently constructed barriers, making it difficult to be an emerging adult in this cultural moment. In the next couple of chapters we turn a corner and look at the life-stage issues that separate young adults from the church and one another. These next couple of walls will have less to do with our cultural moment and would apply to most twenty-somethings in the past few decades.

In this chapter specifically, we will take a look at the wall of self-sufficiency. Leaders who pioneer forged families will inevitably face this barrier along the way.

Naked from the Womb

Tears came on. I couldn't help it. They hit me like a flood. Panic set in and I looked for somewhere I could cry alone. The campus ministry building was packed with students. Hopefully, no one would notice.

I found an open bathroom, lunged inside, closed the door, and groped for the light switch. It took a second for my eyes to adjust as I stared at the paycheck. It still read $200.00 Just two hundred dollars! How was I supposed to live off of that for the rest of the month? Rent, food, and gas charges zipped through my mind as I tried to calculate my expenses against this income.

It was my first job out of college. I graduated the previous May, and we were in the middle of the worst economic depression in thirty years. God had called me to campus ministry, but the job required fundraising. Support was not arriving. I thought more would come in for that month, but I was wrong.

I cried in the bathroom as the shock came and went. Then I went back outside to the crowded lobby area. There was ministry to do, conversations to be had, students to be prayed with. I put on a brave face and walked back into the crowds.

Job from the Bible said, "Naked I came from my mother's womb" (Job 1:21). This is how most people feel starting out after high school or college. They start out fresh. Their circumstances are raw and vulnerable. Life is uncertain and unstable.

The basement floor makes them desperate for the sky rise. Most emerging adults set out from graduation with little finances, a pile of student loans, and entry-level jobs. They will do anything to climb the corporate and financial ladder. They will pay any price to rise out of their perilous position.

Self-sufficiency is a stage-of-life issue for emerging adults. This is not a struggle that popped up and concerned itself with Millennials and Gen Zers specifically. Each generation has had its coming-of-age struggles. Building career, starting a family, and finding a steady place to live are just part of life in your twenties. However, Gen Zers and Millennials are aware of the struggles in a special way.

Gen Z experienced the recession in 2008 at an impressionable age. They are well aware of the difficulty of becoming financially established. Millennials aren't just aware of bad economic climates, they have tried to establish themselves in the workforce through the worst of economic times. Between the housing crisis of 2008 and the pandemic of 2020, Millennials have experienced slower economic growth since entering the workforce than any other generation in US history.[1]

I discipled one Millennial named Luke during his first year out of college. One day he came to me for some financial help. There wasn't much money to his name, and he was really in trouble. Luke was renting from a deadbeat landlord who was not responding to any of his work order requests. He was going to have to spend his own money to pay for the repairs. Worse yet, he came to me on this particular day because his car had just been totaled by a storm.

Luke was fresh out of school and was working a low-paying job. He found himself working crazy hours, being nearly broke, living in a tattered apartment, and a tree had just fallen on his car. He was panicky. Luke was now forced to ride to work with friends and was having to tap into social networks to help him fix his apartment. He felt like a lot of us would feel in his position: ashamed.

Luke felt most embarrassed about the fact that he had to rely on others for help. And let's be honest, a lot of us would feel shame in his position. It's because we see self-sufficiency as a sign of success, and anything short of total independence as a sign of personal failure. Needing help cuts to the core of our independence, which is central to our identity. Luke felt embarrassed that he couldn't provide for himself or for his girlfriend (soon-to-be wife). Anyone who has hit a rough financial stretch in their life can relate. I assured Luke that a lot of people go through situations like these in their emerging adult years. Unfortunately, my reassurance didn't sooth his greatly damaged ego.

Luke wasn't lazy, stupid, or a bad provider. He was just unlucky when starting out his adult life. Most of us can relate to his story. However, Luke had something that a lot of us don't have at that stage in life. He had a network to fall back on. Luke's friends supported him and were happy to do so. Luke felt ashamed of his situation, but his community was eager to help when asked.

Pressure to Succeed

Luke was tempted to live in secrecy (behind the wall of self-sufficiency), by keeping his need to himself. Thankfully, he did not do that!

Forged families are open about their struggles and look to meet any needs that others have. Strong young adult communities will break through the wall and exhibit deep levels of vulnerability and a willingness to serve one another.

But why does this seem so difficult to establish? Why do we sometimes struggle to bring young adults together in a deep and bonded way? Well, the wall of self-sufficiency is really strong. The need to look perfect keeps us from being dependent on one another.

Power. Possession. Status. We grasp ahold of these masks instead of truly accepting the vulnerable parts of ourselves. We isolate ourselves by accumulating wealth and status in an effort to keep from feeling weak, unsuccessful, or unwanted. The wall of self-sufficiency is built so we can give off the vibe that we are in control of our own lives. We hide our deepest shame and fears behind our outward appearance.

Money and power-grabbing are forms of image management. The rich seem to be able to live without material need and appear to live without relational need as well. They appear powerful and in control. The temptation to chase riches or to be successful at any cost is not new to emerging generations. It has been a temptation since the beginning of time. Each generation has had to deal with the wall of self-sufficiency when it matures into adulthood.

For young adults, social media influencers are the gold standard of self-sufficient and carefree people. They are expert image-builders. Social media influencers live the life of wealth and freedom that most of us want in our early twenties.

You can find influencers on private jets, in five-star hotels, or eating Michelin-star meals. They are people who gain social media followers by living lavish lifestyles. They represent young money and young freedom. Influencers have hundreds of thousands of followers who are attracted to them because their lives are extravagant. Companies pay influencers huge amounts of money to have their products featured on their lifestyle accounts. These social media stars use their marketing riches to continue living a lavish lifestyle of freedom that attracts followers and fans. This, in turn, generates more big-time marketing money . . . and so the cycle continues.

Hundreds of millions of people are seduced into these accounts because they exemplify the kind of freedom we all crave. We all want the money and power to be self-made. Yet this self-formation leads us into isolation. Money makes it so we don't have to rely on anyone else. Money keeps us from needing to make commitments to others. We don't bond together with other people because we won't need their help. Social media influencers symbolize this kind of independent lifestyle.

Most emerging adults are far from having the kind of independence that social media influencers have, but the alluring lifestyle tempts us into isolation. Dostoyevsky describes how self-sufficiency isolates people in his book *The Brothers Karamazov*. A wealthy, mysterious, and elderly man says this about the appeal of self-sufficiency and isolation:

> [I]solation prevails everywhere. . . . Everyone strives to keep his individuality as apart as possible, wishes to secure the greatest possible fullness of life for himself; but meantime all his efforts result not in attaining fullness of life but self-destruction, for instead of self-realization he ends by arriving at complete solitude . . . for he is accustomed to rely upon himself alone and to cut himself off from the whole; he has trained himself not to believe in the help of others, in men and in humanity, and only trembles for fear he should lose his money and the privileges that he has won himself. Everywhere in these days men have, in their mockery, ceased to understand that the true security is to be found in social solidarity rather than in *isolated individual effort*.[2]

Overworking at Work

Pastors often complain about youth sports keeping children out of church. Work has the same effect for young adults. The quest for independence seduces Millennial and Gen Z adults into ignoring all other aspects of life, including friendship and family.

They can easily become engrossed in their efforts to achieve security through *isolated individual effort.* They often get a bad rap in the workplace, being perceived as lazy or entitled. But those are misinformed stereotypes.

Millennials aren't lazy; they simply want more flexibility than the traditional nine-to-five allows.[3] And Gen Z is characteristically hungry for success. As mentioned earlier, the 2008 recession hit them at a critical time of development, and they aren't naive about the effort it will take to achieve success.[4]

If you want to build a young adult Christian community, then you must combat this all-consuming passion. After interviewing thousands of Millennials, Christian Smith had this to say:

> The central, fundamental, driving focus of life for nearly all emerging adults is getting themselves to the point where they can "stand on their own two feet." Life's major challenge for them is transitioning from dependence to independence, from reliance on others to self-sufficiency, from being under others' authority and eye to living on their own. Emerging adults know that life is not easy, and many are learning that it is even harder than they expected. . . . So successfully getting themselves up on their own two feet, without the ongoing help of parents and others, is the ever-present and overriding challenge of life.[5]

Young adults are haunted by the gap between their current status and financial independence. And they will go to any lengths to close it.

Workplaces take advantage of this desperation. Employers realize that young people are willing to push past healthy work/life boundaries to get ahead. Law practices are especially notorious for this. Senior lawyers in a firm will often allow the younger men and women to work insane hours while they take it easy. Management gets away with power imbalance because of inexperience and general naivety of people in that age bracket. They realize that young adults are willing to work till exhaustion in order to build a career. This isn't just true of law firms, but this happens in the sales world, the finance world, and the ministry world as well.

Winston Churchill once reflected on his twenty-two-year-old self. It is obvious from his quote that he worked tirelessly in order to establish himself and to become free from the bonds he had with other people. He said this:

> I realized there was no freedom without funds. I had to make money to get essential independence; for only with independence can you let your own life express itself naturally. To be tied down to someone else's routine, doing things you dislike—that is not life—not for me. . . . So I set to work, I studied, I wrote. I lectured. . . . I can hardly remember a day when I had nothing to do.[6]

Churchill used workaholism to attain independence and freedom. It motivated his choices in early adulthood.

The Gap between Capacity and Calling

Authors Plass and Cofield wrote: "We are estranged from others because we cannot shake our exaggerated *self-reliance* and *self-preoccupation*. Our relational detachment is sad. We were created for communion and union. But our experience doesn't match what we long to experience."[7]

We each have needs that can only be met by others regardless of whether the need is financial, emotional, or spiritual. This shouldn't cause any of us to feel shameful because every person has some area in their life that requires help from another. No one person is an island. No one person has a completely controlled or stable life on their own. It is not a sign of weakness to need help. It is a sign of your humanity.

Regardless of age, God has a calling on your life that you can't fulfill on your own. The heroes and heroines of Scripture weren't lone rangers. They needed others to complete their God-given callings. The people of Scripture didn't fly solo. David needed Jonathan. Timothy needed Paul. Jonah needed the whale. Even Jesus wanted help from Peter, James, and John at Gethsemane. Each of them wanted and accepted help from others (except for Jonah). We need other people because we are designed to thrive in relationships. "We cannot reach our potential without healthy relationships. Like an acorn maturing into a mighty oak, we grow into maturity through healthy relationships."[8]

A story from Moses' life shows this principle. Moses was an incredibly skillful and heroic leader. God handpicked Moses as the Hebrews' leader. He helped guide them out of Egypt, ushered in the ten plagues, was instrumental in parting the Red Sea, and talked God into staying with the Hebrew people during their forty-year wandering in the desert. Let's just say that Moses was a boss. He ended his life as an accomplished leader with an impressive résumé. But even Moses had limits. He was human. Moses (like each of us will at times) experienced a gap between his *capacity* and his *calling*.

God called Moses to lead the Hebrews out of Egypt and into the promised land, but Moses could not accomplish that on his own. He reached the capacity of what he could carry by himself. Things came to a head when his father-in-law, Jethro, came to visit him in the desert. Moses, at that point, played the role of prophet and king for the Hebrew people and he wasn't accepting help from anyone in his duties. He was governing the Hebrews, which meant he was overseeing every legal dispute that was occurring in their group.

Leading an entire nation can create some really huge stress, especially if done alone. Moses' attention was divided, and he reached the end of his leadership capacity. His father-in-law, Jethro, saw that he was trying to maintain some fairly unrealistic self-expectations. Moses was a burned-out leader and Jethro offered him some fatherly advice.

Jethro saw the load that Moses was carrying and said to him, "What you are doing is not good. You and these people who come to you will only wear yourselves out. The work is too heavy for you; you cannot handle it alone" (Ex. 18:17–18 NIV). Moses wisely heeded his father-in-law's advice and sought out help from others.

Moses created new leadership roles so that other people could take on his responsibility. He delegated and shared his leadership. He asked for and accepted help. These newly empowered leaders helped to oversee the legal disputes within the Israelite community.

Moses needed others to fill the gap between his capacity and his calling. He became a healthier person and leader when he asked for help. This story works as a great leadership principle, and it works extremely well as an example of how we could encourage young adults to humble themselves in times of need.

Emerging adults are always considering the call that God has on their life. On their own, this is a daunting and darkening task. Within community, it is an adventure toward an achievable destination. You can help them fulfill their calling with the help of a forged family.

Playing the Role of Jethro

Jethro knew from experience that it was impossible for Moses to carry the weight of responsibility on his own. Calling is designed to only be achieved together—together with God and together with others. Those who try to fulfill their calling by being a hero will burn out, just like Moses.

Mature Christians can play the role of Jethro in the lives of young believers. Too many emerging adults carry the weight of adulthood on their shoulders alone. They have neither the perspective nor the experience to understand how unhealthy workaholism, materialism, and hero-like striving can be. You can model for them a better lifestyle.

Interdependent Christian communities are thriving Christian communities. Christ is never more present than when we meet each other's needs. Forged families serve each other and look out for one another's needs. Jethro coached Moses to adopt a life-style of interdependence. You can play this same coaching role in emerging adult lives.

Carving Out Sabbath Space

Some emerging adults do have the innate ability to see beyond the blinders. Kyle Martin is one such person. He was a Gen Z high school senior who challenged the wall of self-sufficiency in a viral valedictorian speech. He mentioned it felt good to be named valedictorian of his class. Then, his speech took a left turn. He admitted that the work he put into becoming the top of his class had robbed him of what was most valuable in life. He came to a realization that:

> Working hard is good, it is in fact biblical. But it should not be done for the sole purpose of a goal-sake at the expense of relationship with others. The stress of this year, this goal, and this five-minute speech was paid for with a lack of attending to relationships in my life. . . . I am glad that I have only made the mistake of striving for something that in the light of eternity is not important for just one year. I can't imagine if I had learned this at fifty or at the end of my life.[9]

Kyle worked hard and accomplished his goal at a young age, but walked away with regrets because he didn't attend to the relationships that were most important to him. He learned the value of friendship in the aftermath of success. This is a lesson for all of us in the church to exemplify, regardless of age.

We must continually remind emerging adults that financial and career success are not the greatest values they attain. We know that there is something much more fulfilling. That is the gift of friendship.

Healthy friendships require margin. You must have emotional availability and free time before you can invest in relationships. These are resources that young adults seem to lack. If you help them create margin, then you will help them create community.

The key tool in your belt for carving out margin in the life of a young adult is Sabbath. Individualism makes us the hero of our own story. In it, we must be the achievers and providers. Sabbath flips that story on its head.

Taking one day a week to be unproductive and restful is an act of faith. It tells God that we trust him for our advancement and our well-being. It signals to him that we recognize our own humanity. We are limited, and our lives are in his hands. The simple sacrifice of time allows us to trade in our human potential for God's potential.

Forged families rest together. Rhythms of rest prioritize relationship with God and others above success. Christian communities that practice Sabbath are attractive to emerging adults. These generations will be quick to recognize the life-giving potency of Sabbath.

God yanked me out of unhealthy workaholism in my mid-twenties and dropped me into Sabbath rest. I was working full-time and in seminary full-time. The Holy Spirit kept telling me in prayer to practice the Sabbath. I ignored this prompting and was quick to let the Holy Spirit know I was too busy to rest. After all, ministry is a matter of ultimate importance. Then one day a friend shared with me a dream. He said, "I had a dream about you last night, Austin. You came to me and told me how important the Sabbath had become to you." That was the breaking point. I began practicing weekly rest and have not looked back.

Now, I thank God that Sabbath is a command: "Remember the Sabbath day, to keep it holy" (Ex. 20:8). Observing the Sabbath was a first move for me toward emotional and relational health in my twenties. I began experiencing joy. My marriage immediately improved. I had space to dream once again!

Sabbath isn't the command of a stuffy God who is trying to tie us down and control us. It is the command of a loving God who recognizes the need we have for countercultural rest and relationship.

Earlier in this chapter I mentioned that one major reason emerging adults are not in church is that they see no practical need for religion. Nothing could be further from the truth. Their world is one of workaholism, isolation, insecurity, distraction, and disembodied relationships. These rhythms are ripping the humanity out of our young adults. Yet, Christianity holds within its doctrine the picture of a flourishing life. We hold the truth that can set them free. Give to them the rhythms of rest and they will step into new life with God and with others. Their chains will fall off and they will be restored in relationship.

Emerging adulthood is the perfect stage of life to lean fully into the radical rhythms of rest. Forged families that practice the Sabbath will likely be made up of healthy and whole people. Your emerging adults will have time to share life with one another, to dream together, and to enjoy life. A Sabbathing community will topple the wall of self-sufficiency.

CHAPTER FIVE

The Wall of Transition
Being Steady to Root Faith

I enjoyed coming and going without telling or explaining,
being free. I enjoyed listening without talking. I enjoyed
being wherever I was without being noticed. But then
when the dark change came over my mind, I was
in a fix. My solitariness turned into loneliness.
—Wendell Berry, *Jayber Crow*

Setting Sail

Transition is the single largest challenge to forging a family with emerging adults. They are always on the move. It will sometimes feel like you are saying hello and goodbye to them in the same breath. Internships, college programs, discipleship experiences, gap-year travels, and job changes keep this age group on the move. How can you impact them when they are always on the verge of leaving your city? This chapter will explore that question. Answering it will help us bring them into community, where they can sink down deep roots of belonging.

It has been said that Jesus' most impressive miracle was having twelve good friends in his thirties. The joke rings all too true for many people on the other side of their twenties. Emerging adulthood is filled with transition, and change puts a large strain on relationships.

Each time you move locations it shakes your friendship stick, making it hard for you to hang onto friends. Graduations shake this stick hard. High school graduation launches friend groups into all different corners of the world, and college has the same effect.

I went to a small liberal arts college and had a distinct moment of awareness about graduation during my senior year. I remember sitting in my spring-semester dorm room thinking about all the friendships that I had developed over the last four years. I realized that none of my friends lived together, and our leases were all up after graduation. Come May, we would spread across the state and the country.

That's when reality set in. Graduation would be a huge shake of the friendship stick and I was about to lose many close companions. Diploma day came and went, and I left many relationships behind me when I walked off campus. This was the beginning of a series of major transitions in my twenties. Each one strained my friendships.

Things like graduations, marriages, newborns, job changes, and moving cities have a way of jettisoning people out of our lives. This has been the reality for every generation during young adulthood. Change is simply part of finding the right job, the right house, and the right spouse.

Life transition during these years is nothing new. But Millennial and Gen Z generations have to manage some heightened forms of daily and digital transition. Our increasingly fluid lifestyles are disrupting relationships like never before.

We're on a Boat

Change also affects a person's emotional and spiritual well-being. It can destabilize every part of a person. Those coming into emerging adulthood are already vulnerable. Most people don't start out with set careers or significant others and probably aren't property owners. All of these things help to stabilize people in adulthood, but it takes time to get them established. Young adults typically do not have the luxury of stability.

They are rather like a lone sailor on a sailboat, trying to reach steady ground. They may set a course, and know where they want to go, but there aren't many who make it to a firm destination without some turbulence.

Their sailboat will be hit with waves. Squalls will disorient them. Their boat will be rocked, maybe flip it around, and they will have to set new courses of action. When this happens, they will be confused. They will emotionally struggle to handle the bumps that cause rerouting.

Transition keeps the young adult boat swaying. Life transition, daily transition, and digital transition are three types of waves that can crash in on them, disorient them, and force them to change directions. It challenges their friendships. Learning how to traverse these waves with excellence is a key to building emotionally, spiritually, and relationally healthy community for emerging adults.

Wave 1: Life Transition

It might help us to start with the facts. The average American moves every five years.[1] That number is probably higher for people in their twenties because they average four job changes in the first decade after college.[2] Millennials are notoriously quick to switch jobs or careers, with 21 percent having changed jobs in the last year alone.[3]

The numbers do not lie. Life transition is a big barrier to forging family. Author Robert Putnam wrote in his book *Bowling Alone*: "People who expect to move in the next five years are 20–25 percent less likely to attend church, attend club meetings, volunteer, or work on community projects than those who expect to stay put."[4]

Young adults sacrifice community and change locations for the sake of advancement. Getting to stable life ground seems to be the number-one priority for anyone who finds themselves in the sailboat. Young adults form a full-on obsession with achieving the markers of a mature life. They see every job, city, and relationship as a stepping-stone to getting to stable land.

Advance. Advance. Advance.

The belief is that you must break up normal in order to move forward in life. If you're not changing, then you're not reaching the fulfillment of your dreams. This mindset leads young adults to constantly ponder the next job, city, relationship, house, etc. They stay ready to move to grasp ahold of a better life.

Tech and online addiction help to feed their desire for change. There is no end to online options that they believe will help carry them to success. Apps like LinkedIn, Zillow, and Tinder keep them fixated on the changes they can make to improve their lives. These apps remind them that there is always another upward movement to be made that they're not making.

Lifestyle browsing puts advancement at the tip of their fingers. Yet it also gives them an extreme sense of separation anxiety. Separation anxiety is traditionally thought of as a term to describe how a child feels when they are separated from their mother, but emerging generations feel anxiety about the separation between their current lives and their idealized destination. These apps keep them panting for the perfect life scenario. LinkedIn dangles promotions and careers in front of their eyes. Zillow floods them with pictures of the homes that they could one day afford. Tinder and other dating apps suggest all kinds of people they could date in order to find happiness.

Anxiety and dissatisfaction keep them moving. Pete Greig once commented about the transitory lifestyle of Gen Z:

I see this generation missing their lives in one-year incre-
ments, because there is such a fear of committing to
particular places and contexts. FOMO. It's a real thing.
The trouble is that if you don't commit to certain relationships, tribes, or locations then you just move from place
to place and relationship to relationship. After ten years,
you're like a ghost. But if you're willing to commit and
dig into relationships in particular places; go through
the cycles of illusionment and disillusionment; what
happens is that you begin to build something eternal.
There's a humility in it. The Benedictine vow of stability
is a promise to a place. We are so transient in our relationships and geographies, chasing the next thing and the
greener grass; and you find out it isn't always better in
other contexts.[5]

Job and location transition challenges our ability to connect
deeply with other people—regardless of what age we are—and
keeps us from digging deep roots down in a local community. In
Greig's words, transition in our twenties can make us *ghosts*. That's
a ghoulish word, but it communicates a scary truth. Movement
makes us unknowable. Young adults who constantly move will
become passers-through, with no concrete impact in the places
where they land.

Wave 2: Daily Transition

I remember freshman move-in day at college. I was thrown into
a dorm that was too old, too small, and too overused. The rooms
seemed too tiny, and the roommate situation seemed too . . . inva-
sive. At the time, decorating our rooms was a big deal, but now it
seems like kind of a joke. There wasn't space for anything more
than my bed, clothes, and dresser, so posters on the wall were as

decorative as we were going to get. I still remember meeting the guys on my hall during move-in.

My next-door neighbor Dustin asked me to come over to help him install extra shelves in his closet. That was the beginning of a lifelong friendship. I met another lifelong friend, Will, in the bathroom—the only one on the hall. I met my friend Chris when he invasively poked his head into my room and asked me about my movie collection.

Campus was small and the student population wasn't overwhelming, so the guys on my hall ran into each other at class, the cafeteria, the gym, and just casually walking around. It wasn't long before we gathered nightly to watch movies, play board games, and cause some casual trouble.

Community is birthed from shared space and shared experience. That was the case for my college dorm mates. Our little family forged because we shared the same dorm and campus and did all our activities together. We had everything in common for four straight years, so those friendships developed into deep lifelong companionships.

Knowing people and being known by people—where you are physically—is a massive part of forging a family. The second wave is called daily transition because sometimes we choose not to engage the people who surround us in our everyday lives.

We all live somewhere. But how many of us know the people who live next door? Getting to know the people around us takes courage and initiative, but is absolutely worth the effort.

Can we name our next-door neighbors? Or if we can name our neighbors, do we know where they work or any other details about their lives? We come to and from our homes, travel in and out of the neighborhood, and walk the streets around us, all the while never knowing the people who share our physical space.

Wendell Berry described the wave of daily transition through his character Jayber Crow:

By the time I had got to Lexington, I was so convinced of the temporariness of any stay I would ever make in this world that I hadn't formed any ties at all. At the trotting track and at the shop, I made acquaintances, but I didn't make any friends. At the university I came and went almost without speaking to anybody. Maybe I did and have forgot, but I don't remember eating a meal with another soul during the year and about ten months I stayed in Lexington. For a long time I liked it that way. I enjoyed coming and going without telling or explaining, being free. I enjoyed listening without talking. I enjoyed being wherever I was without being noticed. But then when the dark change came over my mind, I was in a fix. My solitariness turned into loneliness. When I was alone those images moved and Aunt Cordie's voice sounded in my mind, and I couldn't stop them. What I had thought was the bottom kept getting lower in little jerks. When I cried it was getting hard to stop.[6]

Jayber experienced a wave of transition when his solitariness turned into loneliness. He was in a town that he left soon after and didn't get to know the people who surrounded him. Jayber was content with his relationship-free way of life until he was forced to deal with pain in isolation.

That is the experience of emerging generations today. They are surrounded by people but are seen and known by no one. Take, for example, the college campus. It is too often just the place where thousands of individuals gather to pursue their personal interests. Students pass by without saying a word or might live one room away without ever getting to know one another. They share space but their years on campus are a means to an end, not a destination. The temptation is to resist relationships in their physical location.

Or think about the urban cities, where we pass one another every day, but struggle to develop friendships. A pastor in London recently told me, "There are millions of people in this city, but everyone is lonely and riddled with anxiety. It is very difficult to get to know others here. People have just come to accept that crippling anxiety is part of living in the city." Their sailboats are rocked in the wake of people who are constantly moving past them. They are sensed but unnoticed, perceived yet undesired.

Wave 3: Digital Transition

Weighty community is formed through shared space and shared experience, but modern tech challenges that time-tested principle. The rise of social media has changed what friendship means in today's world.

Proximity was once a requirement for friendship. However, you no longer need to be physically around people to communicate with them. Virtual proximity is taking precedence over physical proximity in making and maintaining friendship. Social enclaves have developed where people gather and connect around niche interests online. Things like baking forums, virtual reality gaming clubs, and political blogs are popular places to go to meet people who share similar interests.

It is also normal to have friends that are entirely maintained digitally. I know people who have constant connection with their college friends ten years after graduation, but who don't have fresh relationships with the people in their neighborhoods. I also know people who stay constantly connected with out-of-state family, but struggle to make friends in their own city. We are at risk with replacing analog relationships with digital interaction.

Virtual proximity makes it so that we no longer rely on our physical space to make friends and connect with like-minded people. Bauman Zygmunt wrote: "The advent of virtual proximity renders human connections simultaneously more frequent and more shallow, more intense and more brief. Connections tend to be too shallow and brief to condense into bonds."[7]

If our community life is exclusively online, then we will miss out on full-bodied friendships and the benefits of deep, bonded relationships.

Social media is the community of the distant. It takes us from everyday life and connects us in non-tangible ways with people who aren't near us. It transitions us from our physical space and puts us in a world that surrounds our minds and not our bodies.

The wave of digital transition crashes against the sailboat when emerging adults fail to make bonds and share experiences with people who are physically close to them. They—like many of us—may try to secure emotional and relational health through an abundance of online interactions, but those interactions are unsteady compared to the ones they could have with the people who surround them physically. They will float through young adulthood alone without the anchor of physical friendship.

Rooted Faith

A pastor who does ministry with de-homed people in recovery recently told me, "The population we serve is transient and constantly on the go. We average one to two years with them from the time they walk through our doors. For instance, last year we baptized 89 new people into faith. Today, there might be one to two dozen of those people still in our church. It's just the reality of the population. We have to think about growing them deep in God quickly, because the time we have with them is short."

The de-homed and recovery community faces unique challenges, but they share one commonality with the average emerging adult: they are transient and on the go. It is worth thinking about how to flash fry community with young adults, given the fact that any of us may only have a couple of years with most of them. We need to help them quickly grow deep relationship roots. Ephesians 3:14–19 says:

> For this reason I bow my knees before the Father, from whom every family in heaven and on earth is named, that according to the riches of his glory he may grant you to be *strengthened* with power through his Spirit in your inner being, so that Christ may dwell in your hearts through faith—that you, being *rooted* and grounded in love, may have the strength to comprehend with all the saints what is the breadth and length and height and depth, and to know the love of Christ that surpasses knowledge, that you may be filled with all the fullness of God. (emphasis added)

If we can help emerging adults grow deep roots, then the rest of their lives can produce good fruit. In the passage Paul is sharing a prayer with the Ephesians that encourages them to be rooted and strengthened in the love of God. A person's twenties are the prime time of life for that to happen. Paul asks that "you" be strengthened, and "you" be rooted in love. An interesting part of this passage is that this is a plural "you," meaning *you all* or *you guys.*

It's a request given to people who are growing deep roots in community together. Growing deep in God can happen in isolation, but family-like community helps stabilize our lives so that we can root ourselves deep in healthy soil.

As leaders, we can facilitate forged families for the emerging adults that end up living on our streets, our neighborhoods, and in our cities. In this way, we can help them anchor spiritual roots into our communities.

Here are some intentional ways that we can forge family for those who pass through our area.

Tips for Intentional Forged Family

Tip 1: Provide Living Space

Emerging adults are always looking for a new place to live. Month-to-month and yearly leases keep them in a loop of searching for bed space.

Do couples or families in your church community have extra bedrooms or basements that they can rent out to people who need them? Are there landlords in your church that can provide houses for communities of young adults to live within?

These spaces don't have to be free to be effective. They just have to be available. Newcomers would be interested in living communally with others if they simply knew of a way to make that happen. The largest uphill struggle for this will be finding the initial locations and helping to form the first groups to move in. These rented houses and beds have a way of staying within the same Christian communities from generation to generation. You can point newcomers to these homes as a way of helping them to root within your city and church.

Tip 2: Live in the Same Neighborhood as Your Church and Workplace

Encourage emerging adults to synchronize the places that they most often commute between: work, grocery, gym, home, etc. If they choose to work, live, and worship in a single neighborhood then they will find it easier to build common experience with others and a forged family will arise out of everyday life. These spaces will act in chorus with one another and help us to develop meaningful relationships.

I have lived in the same neighborhood for the last eight years. I always say that the neighborhood committed to me before I committed to it. It is an urban area where I can walk to the grocery store and church, and I have a selection of great coffee shops within strolling distance.

These dynamics shrink large and unwelcoming cities into smaller ecosystems where you have the chance of getting to know the people who surround you. It took a year or two, but now I know the homeless people who live in the park and the older men who frequent my Starbucks and my gym, and I unintentionally run into people from church on a daily basis. These friendships quickly arose, and it has since made it hard for me to leave. From a church leader perspective, it's important to notice the young adults in your neighborhood. The shared space is good ground for cultivating relationship.

Tip 3: Encourage Decision-Making with a Communal Lens

C. S. Lewis once said, "Friendship is the greatest of worldly goods. Certainly to me it is the chief happiness of life. If I had to give a piece of advice to a young man about a place to live, I think I should say, 'sacrifice almost everything to live where you can be near your friends.'"

We live in a fluid society, but what if community took a higher priority in the moves that emerging adults made? No one would question a young person for moving to a better job or a bigger house. But they would get some strange looks if they chose to move somewhere for a church or for a group of friends.

Our day and hours demand that we reprioritize community in the decision-making process. Each of us needs to view life decisions through a communal lens. Jon Tyson wrote: "One way to do this is to process our life choices through a communal lens, one that takes into consideration the effect of our choices—not just on our families but on our church and community.[8]

Do young adults chose to move location, or to stay, based on how it impacts their community, and vice versa? I am hearing more and more stories of people who are choosing to stay or leave based on the way it impacts their community. A recent college grad recently told me that he decided to leave a great job in Illinois to move to Detroit to be close to a father-like mentor. I also have good friends who have passed up work opportunities to stay in the communities where they are involved. Seeing decisions through a communal lens will challenge the priorities of success and mobility that keep people from forging family in their twenties.

Transition is inevitable in the world in which we live. The waves of life transition, daily transition, and digital transition can rock our boats and make us feel like we are in unsteady water. The good news is that Christian community and the local church can help steady the ship and provide a safe passage to a stable life. Emerging adulthood is the prime time of life to be strengthened, be rooted, and grow deep in the love of God. Forged family creates healthy soil for roots to sink into, and with the help of Christian community, young adults can reach a full adult life bearing good fruit.

INTERMISSION

Heard—Healed—Restored

TEARS WELLED UP IN HER EYES. THE NERVOUS AND sincere college student standing before me had come forward for prayer and tears flowed before her words. The pain showed on her face, and I couldn't help but begin guessing what she would ask prayer for.

This moment came at the end of a monthlong ministry tour where I connected with thousands of students across six states and fifteen different universities. The tour focused on how one can pray for a move of God on the college campus. Each night we shared ministry time with students following the worship service. This young woman had come forward for prayer on the final night of the tour.

Looking at her caused me to recall all the previous prayer requests that I had received throughout the last month. The prayer-request memories flooded my mind. There were many themes that surfaced in that moment. The tour had been a unique glimpse into the prayer closet of emerging adults across the country. As I stood before this brokenhearted girl, the prayers of hundreds of students began to merge into a single desperate cry of a generation.

The student eventually collected herself, looked up toward me, and began speaking. What she voiced that night sounded strikingly similar to the needs of previous weeks. Nearly all of her needs revolved around broken relationships and friendships. She talked about being bullied on a group text thread, having fallouts with family members, and feeling alone. She brought up feeling anxious about the future and how some days loneliness and anxiety made her too depressed to go to class or to work.

She struggled to connect with others. She struggled to get out of bed in the morning.

The prayer requests of this young woman cemented in my mind that loneliness and isolation is the main source of pain for the majority of students. She sobbed trying to talk about her loneliness, anxiety, and depression. She was cripplingly alone.

Getting in the Fast Lane

Self-sufficiency, transition, competition, and distraction are creating barriers between us. Current advances in technology have joined with widespread postmodern individualism to heighten these walls and isolate us from one another. Every sector and category of our society is splintering in a way that silos the individual. Our shared ideologies and life rhythms create a chasm between us.

Today, we find ourselves unnaturally and inhumanly separated. And this separation doesn't come without consequences. We cannot emotionally cope with the lack of nurturing relationships in our lives. Anxiety, depression, loneliness, and desperation are signs of a deep longing that are innately inside emerging generations for relationship.

Many, like the young woman in the story, crave intimacy till we ache.

We've searched to understand the major walls of isolation that separate young adults from the church and each other. Hopefully, we each have a better grasp of how cultural influences take root in and shape their lives.

With the barriers in the rearview mirror, we can now hop on the express lane and consider what journeying with others actually looks like. It is now time to shift our focus from the mechanics of loneliness and to begin considering how to reverse the curse. The remainder of this book will explore God's design for community and how emerging adults can forge families in their twenties.

Answering the Cry

How many students and emerging adults have cried out to God today in their loneliness? Their desperation puts them in good company. We see people cry out to God all across Scripture.

The Israelites cried to God in desperation quite a few times in the Old Testament. One example of this is from Exodus, where the Israelites pleaded with God to end their slavery. They provided for us a beautiful picture of God's attitude toward hurting, broken, and helpless people. The Hebrews faced serious oppression (understatement of the year) as slaves in Egypt.

Their only resolve was to turn to God: "[T]he people of Israel groaned because of their slavery and cried out for help. Their cry for rescue from slavery came up to God" (Ex. 2:23). God then told Moses: "I have surely seen the affliction of my people who are in Egypt and have heard their cry because of their taskmasters. I know their sufferings, and I have come down to deliver them out of the hand of the Egyptians" (Ex. 3:7–8a).

God wasn't deaf. He heard the Israelites' needs and responded. People are pretty familiar with the exodus story, and you probably know the story of how they were rescued from Egypt. God sent plagues, Pharaoh freed the Israelites, and then the Egyptian army perished in the Red Sea.

God hears, God heals, and end of story, right? Well, not exactly. The Egyptian army was defeated and the Israelites were freed, all in the first fourteen chapters of Exodus. But the book is forty chapters long. What about the final twenty-six chapters of the book?

The remainder of Exodus shows that God wasn't only interested in fixing the problem of slavery. He wanted to come down and join the Israelites in the middle of their mess.

God saved them from Egypt, but he was saving them into something they probably didn't imagine. God saved the Israelites into relationship with himself and relationship with one another.

The book of Exodus ends with the freed people of God experiencing his glory. We find God, in the last chapter, dwelling in the middle of his people. He put his glory in a tent, and the tent in the Israelite community. He sat with them as a cloud during the day, and he ruled over them as fire by night. God began speaking intimately to the people of Israel. He guided them relationally and protected them with his presence. God's intimate glory sat in the core of their community.

Exodus shows that God rescued the Israelites in order to live among them and give them an identity as his people. He removed them from a cursed lifestyle and also provided the medicine for their healing. He gave them the Ten Commandments (along with many other lifestyle guidelines) and his presence.

The Israelites were healed from the damage of slavery through the presence and lifestyle of God. It was in these two new blessings that they formed a new identity as a people group. They were no longer slaves; they became the people of God.

The Israelites were a family of God's sons and daughters. He didn't just save, he also restored. The Israelites experienced the renewal. Their example follows a larger pattern throughout Scripture: renewal always includes restored relationships. God established the Israelites in personal identity through deeper relationship with him and with one another.

God heard the Israelites' cries, healed their pain, and restored them into relationship.

Heard—Healed—Restored

Jesus, being God, repeated this pattern many times throughout the Gospels. He heard cries for help, healed the pain, and restored the relationship.

Luke 17:11–19 is an excellent example of this process working itself out in Jesus' ministry. In this passage we find a group of lepers. They're not allowed to be near anyone unafflicted by illness (or "clean") because of their terrible disease. They're considered to be "unclean" by the societal rules of the day, so they are ostracized and required to live outside of the cities in camps for sick people. Talk about being isolated!

One day a group of lepers sees Jesus from a distance. They can't approach him legally because of their disease. So, they cry out to him for help: "Jesus, Master, have mercy on us" (v. 13). So, Jesus did what Jesus does: he healed their disease. Then he sent them to the priest. The priest had the power to declare the lepers clean so they could enter into normal community once again.

Jesus healed the lepers not only so they could be disease-free, but also so they could be restored to relationship with the people of their community. God heard their cries. God healed their pain. God restored them in relationship.

Jesus continues the work of healing and restoring in our world today through the church. Jesus leads the worldwide community of Christians, making them the center of his saving power. Christian community is the community of the once broken—the community of ones who have cried out for help; the community of those restored to the family of God.

Jesus' church operates as his hands and feet in the world today. We are charged to carry on his mission. Those who have been healed and restored are now asked to extend salvation to the world. Jesus looked at the lepers with his eyes, he heard them with his ears, and responded to them with his mouth. Take a second and look at your hands and your feet. Think about what you're hearing and seeing right now. Jesus has made you, as a Christian, his hands and feet in the world today. Jesus' church (his body) is now the chief way he hears, heals, and restores.

Tears That Heal

Tears welled up in his eyes. He struggled to get the words out as the other forty of us waited in the old church sanctuary. It was the last night of spring break and college students were sharing how the trip had impacted them. The group was mostly upper-classmen and campus ministry staff, but this freshman was trying to muster up the courage to speak. It had been a long week and we hadn't heard him talk much.

He was a shy and unassuming newcomer to our group, and had apparently been deeply impacted during the trip. He collected himself at long last and began to talk. His words were simple and, to some, they might have seemed non-profound, but they have stuck with me for many years.

He voiced that he finally found home and belonging within our community that week. It was the first time in his life that he had ever felt accepted by others. He had been a lone ranger. But he forged family during that weeklong trip. This student would return home from spring break within a community of trusted friends.

The community experience during that spring break trip invited him into relationship with God and others. He was not previously a Christian, yet his heart warmed to God throughout the week. The other students listened attentively as he shared what their newfound friendship meant to him. His testimony was simple yet profound, coming from the depths of human longing.

Our little college group listened with reverence and soaked up the authenticity of the moment. His tear-filled testimony carried weight because of its vulnerability. We walked away that night knowing a deep wound in this young man's life had been touched, and that he was healing in relationship.

His tears were tears of healing. They were tears that welled up from the fountain of belonging and flowed to saturate the pain of long-suffering rejection. This student found Jesus' restoration through acceptance in the community. That week marked a new start in his spiritual journey, and he is now entering his second decade of full-time ministry. This student did not just heal from his loneliness. He was restored to relationship with God and relationship to others.

Forged families are human harbors where emerging adults find refuge and restoration within a relationally broken world. The Holy Spirit is attracted to the unity of a group who is bonded together as one. It is within the community of the Spirit where healing takes place. The body of Christ is designed to transform our tears of loneliness into tears of belonging.

The rest of this book will explore the dynamics of a family-like Christian community, the kind of belonging that heals. You will be given the knowledge needed to build environments where forged families of young adults can thrive. You will have a first-hand look at how emerging generations are be restored to God, one another, and the church.

The second part of this book carries the hope of renewal; renewal for the church and renewal for the young. It is time for each of us to move beyond the walls of isolation and into restorative community together.

PART TWO

CHAPTER SIX

Belong Together

What Grabs Your Attention Grabs Your Affection

> *God is not just saving individuals and preparing*
> *them for heaven; rather, he is creating a people*
> *among whom he can live and who in their life*
> *together will reproduce God's life and character.*
> —Gordon Fee, *Paul, the Spirit, and the People of God*[1]

OKAY, SO YOU ARE ALL IN ON THE RESTORATIVE POWER of forged families. You want to knock down the walls of isolation and bring emerging adults together into a family-like Christian community. So, how does that happen exactly? What rhythms mark a community of the Spirit that can transform someone's twenties?

A friend from Australia grew up in a home where God was neither acknowledged nor disavowed. He recently spent a few weeks with our family. At the end he said that he felt closer to our family than to his own. Why? Because we prayed together. He told me, "There is something intimate about praying with your family. It is deeply personal, and I feel really close to you because we pray before meals."

I have good news. Your church holds the keys to intimate community in the simple spiritual practices and the habits of worship—even in praying before meals! In this chapter we will see how spiritual practices within family-like communities shape people. And then we will look at the cadence of the spiritual practices as a way to forge your young adult family together.

Jesus Challenges Identity

It was the strangest altar call I have ever heard. I was in Mozambique at a three-month missions school where evangelism trips in the African bush happened every weekend. It was toward the end of the school, and I was on my final trip into the bush. We visited the local people in a nearby village during the day that was previously unreached by Christians, and a large group of them arrived that night to hear about Jesus.

No one in the community knew who Jesus was or was familiar with the stories in the Gospels. The local government was run by leaders of a different religion, and they kept a tight stranglehold on the lifestyle of the people there. Nevertheless, a crowd of hundreds arrived that night.

The group that gathered was shown a movie about the life of Jesus in their native language. A missionary followed up by giving an invitation to become a follower of the Messiah. "If you choose to follow Jesus then you'll have to give up everything," he said through the speakers. "Your families will reject you; you'll be hated by your neighbors; you will probably be physically attacked."

It was not exactly what I would call a seeker-friendly message. However strange it seemed to me, people responded and came forward. Many walked up that night to become Christians or to receive prayer for healing. Jesus inspired hope within that crowd of people. And the Holy Spirit convicted the hearts of men and women to come to Christ, even in the face of persecution. Those who committed their lives to Jesus that night were no doubt ostracized by their families and their communities. Their choice to follow Jesus was a choice of life and death in more ways than the spiritual.

The beautiful people of Mozambique are not alone in having to choose between Jesus and their families. I have known many young adults who have chosen radical lives for Christ and have risked losing relationships with their mothers and fathers in the process. I have Jewish friends who were cut off from their families when becoming Christians; friends whose atheist parents became indignant when they made faith decisions; and many young adults whose Christian parents have warned them against becoming too invested in their faith.

The choice to follow Jesus is one that threatens family life for many people both inside and outside of the persecuted church. It is certainly not an unfamiliar danger for many young believers in the Western world today.

Hate Your Family?

Luke 14:26 says: "If anyone comes to me and does not hate his own father and mother and wife and children and brothers and sisters, yes, and even his own life, he cannot be my disciple."

In case you're wondering who said the words in Luke, don't be alarmed—be *very* alarmed!

Those are the words of Jesus. This classic tough teaching of Jesus is a head-scratcher. Sometimes I wish Jesus were easier to explain. I mean, I don't try to justify his comments; he's God and has the ability to make the truth claims that he wants. But I do want to try to understand what he meant as best I can.

This is the kind of Jesus teaching that is sometimes misunderstood. Let's not overlook this scripture because it holds special insight into the importance of community for emerging generations. Embrace the awkward with me and take a deeper look.

You have to understand the concept of family in Jesus' time in order to understand this strange (to us) teaching. Family was the strongest source of a person's identity and lifestyle during the time that Jesus was walking the Earth. The people of his day were group-oriented people; they found their identity in the group in which they belonged. Thus, their family group was their main source of identity.

This is hard for us to understand completely in our Westernized individualistic society. We are forced to find our identity in external things and in what we accomplish for ourselves. For example: the money we make, the brands we buy, the clothes we wear, etc. are all ways that we form our identity.

People today aren't identified or categorized first by group or family as was the case in Jesus' culture. We are instead placed into groups within society based on external signals, personal accomplishments, and wealth.[2]

In Jesus' world, *your family determined your lifestyle.*

This tough teaching was not an invitation to be hateful (in the way we think of the word). Families practiced life together. They relied on one another for financial support, safety, security, identity, and belonging. But Jesus taught an upside-down kingdom. Living in that kingdom required radical change in a person's habits and actions.

A Jew who did not reject their family lifestyle could not follow Jesus. If a new convert stayed in their family unit, then they would be held captive to their old identity and old lifestyle, with no real opportunity to follow Jesus. The odd teaching from Jesus about hating your family was a challenge for converts to sacrifice their old patterns of life in order to join him in a fresh identity and a lifestyle of discipleship.

Leaving a family of origin was not an easy process. It was high-risk and painful. However, Jesus did not leave them orphaned. He gave them a new family to belong to—the church. It was a swap, trading in your old family for the community of disciples.

Jesus' tough teaching was an invitation to take on his identity by belonging within his family. Group belonging was the source of identity, so family change was identity change.

This tough teaching is classic Jesus. He has a way of finding and challenging the things that we love the most. He asked the rich young ruler to sell all his possessions (Matt. 19:21). Jesus told another man that, in order to follow him, he had to leave his deceased father and to "let the dead bury their own dead" (Matt. 8:21–22).

The call of discipleship has a way of pinpointing and challenging the things that give us a personal sense of identity and well-being. Jesus wants to find whatever that is, so he can replace it with himself.

For first-century Jews, following Jesus meant replacing family. For us today, it may mean rethinking our sexuality. Sexuality is one area that we often look to in order to define and categorize ourselves. Culture suggests that we identify ourselves as our sexuality: married, single, heterosexual, homosexual, open, closed, affirming, etc. This is the mirror we look in and lens through which we've viewed others since the sexual revolution. For decades now Western-society Christians have been in constant tension with culture over sexual practices. Why is this? At the center of the cultural backlash against Christian sexual ethics is this one issue: *identification.*

Culture has placed sexuality at the core of a person's identity. And yet, Jesus poses a challenge to our highest priorities, whatever they may be. This disturbs culture. It creates anger, angst, and confusion. If sexuality is no longer the first and undisputed leader in personal identity, then we have no way to order the rest of our lives. Sexuality places us in a group, gives us a sense of belonging, and informs us how to live the rest of our lives.

In our culture today, *our sexuality determines our lifestyle.* Removing sexuality from the primary spot of identification creates chaos in our society. It is incomprehensible for many to instead imagine ordering life around the teachings of Jesus.

The call to follow Jesus—regardless of whichever society, generation, or age of the world you live in—is a difficult one.

Becoming Jesus' disciple means coming into his kingdom, the realm where he is king and has authority. He wants to be our first love, the place where we find our sense of identity and belonging, and the person that we rely on for everything. To become a disciple is to allow *Jesus, and his family, to determine our lifestyle.*

Killing off our old loves requires living a new way of life. That's where our Christian family comes into play. Jesus didn't ask people to hate their families without having a new family in mind. He doesn't just rip us from our old ways of living without planting us in a support system for our new kingdom identity and lifestyle.

In the intermission chapter I mentioned that Jesus doesn't just save us from sin, but he saves us into relationship. Jesus saves us into a new family, the family of God. Community is our support system for learning to love Jesus, follow his teachings, and rely wholly on him.

We learn to live under the reign of King Jesus by living life alongside others who also live in his kingdom. It is within this community that we learn how to prioritize God and let our lives flow from him. In essence, *our new family determines our new lifestyle.*

These new family-like relationships imbed us within the rhythms and the presence of Jesus. Churches that neglect to build these relationships will not embed emerging adults within its community, let alone spiritually form them. Young adults may attend for a season, but the church will fail to retain them. Let us not underestimate the cost of discipleship for young Christians.

The lifestyle that Jesus calls twenty-somethings into is too difficult to live out in isolation. The culture offers too much resistance for us to rely on event attendance and a Sunday-morning program to carry the weight of discipleship.

Family-like community is the only disciple-making mechanism powerful enough to bond new converts to the church for a lifelong journey of formation. Only a soul-depth sense of belonging within the church will keep emerging adults within the faith.

They must learn to find their sense of identity within a community of believers, more so than within their sports teams, their college campus, or even their biological families. Their personal sense of self must flow from their relationship with Jesus and their relationships with Christian friends.

We will lose them if we provide anything short of a forged family.

Christian family was Jesus' strategy for retention. It was the Velcro of the early church.

What Grabs Your Attention
Grabs Your Affection

The Acts 2 church was made up of thousands of new converts. It's no coincidence these new believers went straight into Christian community from the waters of baptism. They had to learn their new way of life—and fast. Pagan culture never stopped seducing them, beckoning them back into their old lives.

The apostles were challenged with the task of developing a new identity in the hearts of these three thousand converts. They chose to form these new believers within a family-like community that demonstrated the Way of Jesus.[3]

> And they devoted themselves to the apostles' teaching and the fellowship, to the breaking of bread and the prayers. And awe came upon every soul, and many wonders and signs were being done through the apostles. And all who believed were together and had all things in common. And they were selling their possessions and belongings and distributing the proceeds to all, as any had need. And day by day, attending the temple together and breaking bread in their homes, they received their food with glad and generous hearts, praising God and having favor with

all the people. And the Lord added to their number day by day those who were being saved. (Acts 2:42–47)

New relationships and new life rhythms were given to these new converts. A key formation principle in this strategy is that *your habits determine who you become.*

The baby believers in Acts 2 banded together to become like Jesus through worship and the implementation of his teachings and lifestyle. They practiced Christian habits to become thoroughly discipled Christians.

Our communities will do the same if we hope to thoroughly disciple emerging adults. We must give them family-like Christian community that practices the way of Jesus. This is where they will learn to worship Jesus, to practice his habits, and develop faithfulness amid a hostile society.[4]

It is difficult for anyone to live a godly life on his or her own. A person in isolation is too easily dragged out of Christianity by the tide of secularism. However, a godly lifestyle practiced within Christian community will help anchor a person in their faith. Christian brothers and sisters help us live into a countercultural lifestyle.

We also notice another key formation principle in Acts 2: *what grabs your attention grabs your affection.*

Technology is in an all-out war for our attention. Consider your phone, for example. Your phone is an incredible device, but it's interesting how the phone works. It is one of the most formative inventions in human history. Our phones have the power to form the human heart and mind and, consequently, all of society.

Our phones are basically walking billboards that we carry around with us everywhere. They are devices that we give permission to interrupt our days, nights, and minds. Think about it: How many apps have we given the power to interrupt our days whenever they want?

The tech companies are playing a game to see how long they can suck people into a black hole of surfing the internet and binging media. The other day I went to check the weather. I picked up my phone, ended up surfing for a half hour, put it down, and then I realized that I had never actually looked at the weather. The tech companies think, "Hey, this is really great!" because the more clicks you get, the more you get sucked in, the more ads you'll see, and the more dollars make it into app developers' pockets. In this new attention economy, our attention is mined for money. "Extracting eyeball minutes, the key resource for companies like Google and Facebook, has become significantly more lucrative than extracting oil."[5]

Marketers use apps to capture our attention and they end up making money. We consequently end up seeing thousands of messages a week on our phones. We're formed by marketing messaging, and we don't even realize it; we actually consider it normal.

But what grabs our attention grabs our affection and, in the course of years, we end up being shaped by messaging in ways that we never intended. We never consciously give others access to our hearts, but media ends up shaping our desires, images of the good life, ideals, ideas, etc. Marketers, phone companies, and tech companies have done their jobs when they have altered what we want in life.

Emerging adults—like the rest of us—are being formed by the attention-grabbing seduction of technology. Years of media consumption shape us into people we did not intend to become. Instagram is a great example of this. Ask yourself: *How has Instagram shaped what I desire and what I love?*

I follow two types of people on Instagram. One type of people are my friends. I want to see things like wedding and baby updates from friends. But there is another type of person that I follow as well. These are the people that are living the type of life I want to emulate. These people inform me on how I should live.

Instagram influencers provide a glimpse of a life that I want to live. I will catch myself desiring a pretty selfish lifestyle if I look at

Instagram without a pretty strong internal filter. Instagram is the most classic example of allowing messaging in, seeing something you like, and allowing it to inform you of who you should become.

We should encourage young adults to consider what they give their attention to. Our communities should develop an ethos about screen habits and content consumption. We will lose them to the competing messages on their screens if we don't give them a developed understanding of how to be distinctively Christian in their tech use. How often do we consider what we watch, listen to, and consume? Do we think about the people we follow on Instagram and social media? We should, because we fill our minds with the messages they're sending and the images they're showing, and it ends up forming us into the people we become. What grabs our attention grabs our affection, and we end up becoming what we consume.

Communities help to shape our attention and our affection. We need to encourage people to join family-like community in their twenties that can help shape a lifelong love and adoration for Jesus. College sports show us wonderfully how community helps to shape what we love for life.

I used to work at the University of Kentucky, and the sports culture is king in the city. Every year I would see students come in as freshmen and immediately be captured by the excitement around the football and basketball teams. People camp out for tickets, tailgate, and go crazy at the game. They sing fight songs, do homecoming weekend, and it's the most exciting thing in the city to do with friends. The games are an amazing experience because of the support they get from the city and from the students. Adults, college students, and children alike get excited about these events, and most everyone gets caught up into the hype. These games are hugely emotional experiences between the fight songs, the big momentum plays, and the standing up and sitting down.

I remember my first UK basketball game. The UK point guard hit a turnaround three-pointer to win the game at the buzzer. People freaked out. I think I rode out of that stadium on a cloud. That's what big college (or pro) sports do—they capture our attention and our emotions. Sports events are incredibly formative. Fans end up following sports blogs, sports social media accounts, and joining fantasy football leagues. Sports have the power to shape our lives.

If you ever attend a college football game then take a second to notice how many older men and women, who have been out of college for the last thirty or forty years, are still wearing the exact same game-day gear they were wearing in college. It's thirty years later, and they're still buying team paraphernalia. They're still spending thousands of dollars on tickets, tailgating, and food.

The habits they formed in emerging adulthood—the things they allowed to grab their emotions, attention, and desires—have formed them into a certain type of person. It has not just formed their younger years but has formed them for a lifetime. Sometimes I wonder: How many of my male friends will be more loyal to their sports teams than their wives? How many of us will stick with a sports team for a lifetime but experience divorce? It seems like we have such a loyalty to these things because they captured our attention at an impressionable age.[6]

Space for God

The American church cannot produce enough content to combat the messaging that is produced by secular media outlets. We will not form emerging adults in the faith by winning a war of content creation. Family-like community (and the experience of worship within it) is the only formational tool in the church's hands that is powerful enough to spiritually form new Christians in today's society.

The way of Jesus, when practiced within a forged family, removes formational power from the world and places it in the hands of God. The Acts 2 converts left their old families in order to develop their identity in a new family. This new family-like community lived as Jesus lived, doing the things that Jesus did.

These rhythms are known as spiritual disciplines. Classic Christian disciplines, if given your attention, will form your love for God.

It works like this: going to a football game, standing up and down, cheering, and doing the fight song will turn you into a certain type of fan. Spiritual disciplines will have a similar effect on your spiritual life. They will shape emerging adults' lives and loves for God.

A person's twenties is the perfect time for them to encounter the spiritual disciplines, the exact ones you'll find practiced in the Acts 2 community. These classic Christian practices will create space in a young person's life where they are likely to experience God and be shaped by him.

They are the spaces where God has promised to meet us and shape us in his presence. If we can teach these rhythms to emerging adults, then God will grab their attention and grow their love for him for a lifetime.

Community Rhythms That Shape Us

Privatized religion is a problem for the West, especially within the church.[7] Many—if not the majority of—people who attend church are not comfortable being openly spiritual with others. We struggle to teach the spiritual disciplines to young believers because the older Christians in our churches do not know how to pray in a group, read Scripture with others, or have spiritual friendship.

We most often think about these spiritual disciplines as being solo activities, but God didn't intend for these to only be done in secret! That's why it's important that we put young adults in community spaces where these habits are shared. That is how they will learn to live like Jesus. Life in the kingdom of God is caught as much as taught.

We are going to spend some specific time on the community practices in Acts 2:42—teaching, fellowship, breaking of bread, and prayer. The four spiritual practices presented in Acts 2:42 are special because they are done within a forged family. They show us the power of practicing the spiritual disciplines with others. Let's examine these practices and see how community impacts them.

Acts 2:42 begins: "they devoted themselves to the apostles' teaching . . ." What does the "apostles' teaching" mean? That feels like an old-time Bible phrase. The apostles were the early church leaders who had personally seen or spent time with Jesus. They were the people who could credibly represent his teaching, life, and ministry to others.

The early church gave themselves to this useful teaching and worked out their beliefs together. It's important that we engage with sound instruction and sound doctrine, especially when we're young in the faith. We should encourage others, as well as ourselves, to not only examine Scripture and theology on our own but do it alongside other people as well. Reading Scripture, discerning it, comparing texts, and trying to figure out what God is speaking to you is not a job for an individual in isolation. It is a job for community.

Today we know the apostles' teaching through the words of Scripture. But the disciples, in Acts 2, personally heard teaching from the mouths of the apostles themselves. They followed the apostles' guidance and accepted their words as truth. When the apostles spoke, they did so with authority. Their leadership directed a community of followers.

It's hard to imagine ourselves accepting authority in the way that these disciples did. Receiving leadership makes us feel uneasy, and understandably so! Many of us have been in negative leadership environments and have served under corrupt authorities. If you haven't had an experience with bad leadership in the church or the workplace, then just go to Twitter. If an example is not immediately on your feed, then go to the "trending now" section, and you'll find unlimited real-time examples of leadership gone wrong. You'll find authority abused.

Our culture is brimming full of negative leadership examples, which means we'll have to overcome a natural distrust of leadership to accept a church's teaching on Scripture.

It is actually very important for emerging adults to learn from the teaching of people who know way more about God and Scripture than they do. That is a really tough practice to encourage because of all the negative leadership experiences many of us have had, and because scriptural authority often comes off very dogmatic.

Young adults won't be interested in authority detached from relationship.

But they'll take advice and leadership from older Christians whom they know love them and have their best interests in mind. There is a relational gap that we need to bridge in order to help young adults to accept healthy spiritual authority.

They all want mentors. They want someone to show them the way of life—whether that's someone you can imitate in a profession, faith, or hobby. The only difference between a spiritual mentor and a spiritual authority is relationship. If we can establish loving relationship, then spiritual leadership and the teaching of healthy Christian doctrine will be received.

Acts 2:42 continues: ". . . and the fellowship . . ." *Fellowship* is another churchy word. You might think "come to the potluck after Sunday service," when you think of the word *fellowship*. And who wouldn't like fried chicken and green beans after a Sunday service?

But that's not exactly the fellowship concept you see communicated here in Acts 2. Here you see people spending more time together than a once-a-week gathering. You see a group of people who experience community like family, and that's fellowship.

The forged family like that of Acts 2 lives together and sacrifices for one another. If someone's out of rent money, then they collect money and provide for that person. If someone has medical bills, then they're pooling finances to pay for it. That kind of fellowship and belonging may seem impossible to most of us, but I've seen communities that fellowship like this.

Arise Church (the house church movement I planted) models the principle of generosity. House churches rally to pay for each other's needs on almost a monthly basis. Money is raised for things like car batteries, rent, surgeries, food, etc. Arise micro-communities come together to meet one another's basic needs.

Arise house churches look more like Acts 2 than the Sunday-morning service does in general. We seek to model Acts 2:42 in each weekly gathering. We read Scripture together, pray for each other's healing, and eat together. If someone wants to be baptized, they do it. And, if there's a member of their house gathering that has an expense they can't pay, then the fellowship takes an offering to pay it.

That is Acts 2–type fellowship! It is possible. I've seen it with my own eyes.

I wonder what kind of intimacy the early disciples experienced in their community. I imagine them mourning, laughing, and celebrating together. Their unity fueled the activity of the Holy Spirit in their fellowship. It fed their mission and evangelism.

Outsiders saw how Christians cared for each other, provided for others, and treated one another. This is largely why the early church was really attractive for nonbelievers and grew so quickly.

The twenty-first-century church would be radically attractive to nonbelievers if we had this kind of radical unity and radical love for each other. This is what Jesus meant when he said, "By this all people will know that you are my disciples, if you have love for one another" (John 13:35). Unity and fellowship helped fuel early church growth to the extent that Christianity was the largest religion in the Western world within two hundred years of the initiation of the church.

Emerging adults are hungry for churches that fellowship together like forged families. I was at a college event where we invited people forward for prayer at the end. One person came up and said, "I want you to pray for me. I am missing community right now. I don't feel like I am unified with anyone else." So I prayed for him.

He left and someone else sat down. This next young person in line stepped up for prayer and said, "Hey, I want you to pray for me. I don't have the type of community I need to have right now. I feel like I'm missing out on fellowship."

I thought, *Wow, you don't need prayer, you just need to talk to the guy who came up for prayer before you. You don't need prayer; you just need to get together and hang out!*

That is a funny illustration, but most people (even in church) feel lonely. They long to have an Acts 2 unity and fellowship with other people. However, unity and fellowship with others requires a willingness to sacrifice. No one has intimacy without giving themselves to other people. That's a tough bar to overcome for most people in their twenties. However, they will find it well worth the risk if they get a taste of fellowship within a forged family.

Back to verse 42: ". . . to the breaking of bread . . ." What does it mean to break bread? The early church obviously ate meals together, but *breaking bread* may have a meaning deeper than that. It may communicate a special kind of meal that they shared.

We call this meal by a few names: Communion, the Lord's Supper, or the Eucharist. It is the same meal but is called different names by different Christian streams. The sacrament shared in remembering and taking in the body and blood of Jesus was the most common church practice of worship for the early church.

They celebrated Jesus' life and resurrection through the partaking of bread and wine. They took in the presence of God together. Taking this meal together wasn't a one-off event. It was much more frequent than that. It wasn't like they thought, *Let's do this only on Sunday.*

No, they practiced Communion on Monday and Tuesday and Wednesday, and so on. It occurred any time they broke bread together. Christ and his sacrifice were present within the gathering of his body whenever they joined together for a meal. This may be the one practice, in comparison to all the others, where the historic church was most convinced that God would show up. So they broke bread regularly.

Meals are a key weapon in the forged family arsenal. You cannot have tight-knit community without eating together. The table is the one space that emerging adults are most likely to sit down without a phone or a screen to enjoy the presence of other people. Shared meals are the central activity to any healthy community.

Acts 2:42 concludes: ". . . and the prayers." The disciples asked Jesus how to pray. He didn't send them to their bedrooms to recite a wish list to God. He opened his mouth and began praying right in front of them (Luke 11:1–4; Matt. 6:9–13)! Prayer is both caught and taught.

You will never learn how to pray effectively if you never pray with others. Emerging adults will only catch a vision for prayer if they are in family-like communities committed to seeking God in prayer. I have seen this time and time again. There is hardly a more powerful prayer combination than college students and old intercessors. Christians in their early twenties are consistently *inspired* to a deep prayer life when they see older Christians with a passion for prayer.

David Thomas's work on travailing prayer has been the most impactful of any I've come across. He talks about praying to God with absolute emotional honesty. He often says, "The Bible is totally unfamiliar with casual prayer."

We consistently see people all throughout Scripture and church history cry out to God in anguish and desperation. This is the style of prayer seen in the Hebrides Revival, where groups of farmers and housewives would spend all night in their barns pleading with God to fulfill his promises and save the lives of their children.

This reminds me of the "prayer of faith" that Charles Finney used to talk about in his revival work. We are to pray with absolute honest conviction that God will give us what we ask for if we ask in accordance to his will. We are to pray with honesty, conviction, and in the Spirit of prayer.

Forged families that travail in prayer will set young Christians on a journey of a lifetime of prayer. It is the mundane and emotionally dishonest prayer life of rote religion that they recoil against.

One word of caution for gathering young people to pray: do not schedule prayer for a normal time if you want any college students to attend. Ask them to come to a church building at 7:00 p.m. on a Sunday night, and not a single one will show up. However, if you make prayer an exciting challenge, then you will get many emerging adults to attend. Ask them to meet through the night, or on a mountain top, and they will show up.

Young adults are interested in meeting with the living God. If they encounter vibrant prayer communities, then their hearts will be captured by a passion for prayer.

Forging a family was Jesus' method of forming new Christians, and it should be our method today. Build a community around the spiritual practices, and young adults will bond together while being formed in their faith. Acts 2:42 is a great reference point to find the cornerstone rhythms for your young adult community. Remember these key points as you build your forged family: your belonging determines your becoming and, for emerging adults, their family will determine their lifestyle.

CHAPTER SEVEN

Gather Together

Zoom—The New Noise of Emerging Adult Ministries

*To communicate is primarily about the
exchange of information. To commune is
primarily about the exchange of presence.*
—Jay Kim

ZOOM. IT IS NO LONGER THE SOUND A CAR MAKES. ZOOM has risen above the ping, ding, beep, and buzz to stand alone atop the mountain of useful digital connectivity. These noises used to trouble our in-person relationships. Our face-to-face conversations were constantly interrupted by the blips and blurbs coming out of our devices. These temporary moments of digital distraction marred our physical interactions and strained our in-person relationships.

COVID has changed our perceptions of these digital sounds. It pressed the fast-forward button on internet connectivity. The devices that were once seen as distractions are now viewed by many as relational lifelines. The pandemic *Zoomed* us into the future of networking and disembodied community. It, and many other programs like it, are now in the driver's seat of ministry and spiritual formation efforts for emerging generations.

The debate has shifted, and a new worship war has emerged. We have witnessed a contested argument develop over the last five years about the legitimacy of things like digital church lobbies, prayer chat rooms, and online Communion. I, along with many other church idealists, have resisted the move to a completely digitalized church.

However, COVID did not care about our theological presuppositions. The pandemic forced each of us to stretch our concepts of church to include a new kind of digital belonging.

I remember the first time that digital church was presented to me. I saw a video of a well-known pastor describing his next satellite campus as being *everywhere*: "Wherever you are, that's where church is . . . on your phone." At first, I thought it was a joke, like a *Saturday Night Live* skit. But it became all the too apparent as the video went on that the pastor was as serious as a heart attack.

Digital singing, digital lobbies, digital Communion—it is all available online. Church leaders have since felt the pressure to create digital platforms that incorporate the full church experience. The incentive to do so? Well, we are told that emerging adults are online.

"Gen Z is online. That's where you need to be, or you will miss out on an entire generation." How much truth is there in this statement? The sentiment is driving pastors' ambition to build a digital platform. There is a rush for perfect online church experiences: viral videos, interactive social media pages, and the like.

As a church leader, you have probably felt this worry. Get online or be left behind. But will you miss out on an entire generation if you do not have a perfectly curated TikTok feed or Instagram page?

The answer is no. Certainly, the online space cannot be ignored; emerging adults do the majority of their communicating online. But the internet will not be the foundational platform of the next church renewal. Digital communication may support the move of God, but it will not host it.

Forged families are communities of deep discipleship. They can be created in spaces such as church small groups, house churches, campus ministry cell groups, micro-communities, and the like. Forged families can be found wherever emerging adults are bonded together as an interdependent family in the pursuit of Jesus. They are currently absent from most churches; young adults are starved for them. These forged families thrive on embodied communication—laughter, conversation, food, and shared experiences.

Forged families cannot be hosted online, yet they can be bolstered by digital communication. We cannot completely ignore digital space as a way of engaging one another. That would be like trying to play basketball with one eye covered. Online life is too integrated into our physical world to be completely ignored. Digital space may not be a bedrock foundation of a forged family, but it can provide some scaffolding.

This chapter will not answer all our questions of how to strike the in-person/online balance. But it will outline the influence of digital community on the spiritual lives of emerging adults. You will leave with a greater understanding of how to build forged families that can impact the upcoming generations.

The communication revolution of the last twenty years has changed the way we all relate to each other. The church is still curious what the impact might be on our gatherings and worship. How does digital life shape the discipleship of emerging generations?

Connection without Communion

Jonathan Grant, in his book *Divine Sex,* offers some good comparisons between in-person and online relationships. He says that digital communication gives emerging adults *connection without communion,* and *wide but shallow relationships.*[1]

We can connect with anyone and everyone online: celebrities, shared interest groups, and strangers. We can set notifications on our phones to ping us every time another person reaches out to us through social media, DMs, or text. However, these connections are easily managed at our convenience. We can connect as anonymous people. We choose when we engage. And we can cancel the connection if it's not meeting our needs.

Forged families aren't fueled by mass communication but, rather, by the deep relationships of a committed few. Devoted friendships ensure that emerging adult communities keep running. Yet, relationships hosted online demand little depth or loyalty. The interactions we have with friends online are flighty and noncommittal in nature; they can be engaged at random and then left with ease.

Communities that spiritually form young adults are anchored in a physical location. The classic Christian practices that form people are more potent in person than online. Let's take the practice of confession, for example. Christians and non-Christians alike find it easier to confess their sins to strangers online. Digital anonymity makes it easy to tell your story to the world.

The veil of the computer screen seems to encourage us to share our guilt to the world because it blocks us from true intimacy. There is a wide range of people on social media and confessional sites that we can express our guilt to, and who may respond with sympathy.

A confession that once might have been made within the bounds of friendship, family, or church now takes place with no bounds or bonds at all. It goes out to whoever is on the site.

Is this confession? Yes, but not the kind that will shape a young adult into the person God desires them to become. No church leader would suggest that venting to strangers online about our wrongdoings is an adequate expression of confession. But it illustrates a principle: we can segment digital spaces and friendships for certain activities, and exclude these same people from the other areas of our lives.

Social media and online ministry allow us to maintain a broad range of relationships; relationships that we can keep at bay if needed. Digital connectivity is good for wide and shallow relationships, but not as good at stewarding deep, spiritual friendship.

Confession with face-to-face friends is difficult, yet it is the kind of confession that transforms a person by the power of God. Admitting your faults to a friend can hurt. It's like the incision of a surgical scalpel. It cuts and burns, but the spiritual sickness within us is removed.

If an in-person confession or apology is given, then the consequences of actions are dealt with in real time. Conversation and resolution have to happen; there is no blocking, deleting, or ghosting that can occur. We are forced to face the consequences of our actions (quite literally).

Confessing to a friend might bring disapproval. But disapproval, while hard to take, can be part of an ongoing and sustaining relationship. It can mean that someone cares enough to consider your actions and talk to you about their feelings.[2]

It is hard—if not impossible—to host committed communities of presence online. Forged families are nourished by *commune*-ity. Jay Kim wrote: "To communicate is primarily about the exchange of information. To commune is primarily about the exchange of presence."[3] Digital platforms can carry the weight of communication, but not of presence and commitment.

Emerging adults are starved for friends to commune with. Forged families leverage the power of presence for the kingdom. Meet in person, and you may see young adults powerfully formed by practices like confession, prayer, and acts of service.

Holistic Formation

The greatest commandment is to love God with all your heart, and with all your soul, and with all your strength, and with all your mind (Matt. 22:37; Deut. 6:5). This is the great formational task of church leaders as they disciple and apprentice Christians in upcoming generations. The cultural tides are too strong for us to think of spiritual formation as just the passing on of intellectual knowledge.

The internet is good for the transformation of information; it can help develop the mind. But Jesus did not ask the mind alone to grow in deep love for God. He also commanded the heart to passionate devotion, the soul to unabridged longing, and the strength of the body to full surrender for the love of God. This is full-bodied, incorporating every part of the person . . . making it difficult to pastor communities into a holistic love of God in a detached online space.

Nothing other than a full-bodied love for God will suffice for emerging generations to maintain their faith into mature adulthood. Too long the church has relied on worldview as the answer for embedding young believers in faith: "If we can get them to think in the right way, with a Christian lens, then they will be able to discern the right and wrong in the world for themselves." This worldview experiment is failing.

Emerging adults are leaving the church in droves. We cannot drill worldview and theology deep enough within them to stave off the appeal of other ways of thinking. Teaching worldview is a top-down educational approach to formation that stops in the mind and goes no further. We need to move beyond that approach with emerging adults.

My fear with digital ministry is that it is limited. Online communication is a great tool for transferring information, but it is not as good of a tool for full-bodied experience with the presence of God and the presence of other people.

You engage the internet with your mind, but not your body. The church has too long been guilty of filling people's minds while leaving their hearts empty and their spirits starved. We have presented God in truth, but not in experience. We must teach upcoming generations to love God with their whole being, including their affections. This is a near-impossible task for a communication medium like the internet.

We cannot disciple emerging adults solely through a screen and expect them to love God with all their heart, soul, mind, and strength. Church on the internet leaves them holding a bucket of information about God. God is not a concept to be talked about, but a person to be known. What is needed for full-bodied spiritual formation is an experience of the presence of God. And God's manifest power is something that we receive with our whole selves.

Barna recently unearthed five markers of resilient discipleship in the lives of young Christians. The first marker of resilient disciples is that they experience *conversational intimacy with Jesus.*[4] Meaning, God acts on them. They experience God, not as an idea, but as a present reality.

God's presence is felt or at least acknowledged by resilient disciples. To them, God is not just a philosophy or a moral code. The love of God is not just a detached intellectual experience of the mind. No. The love of God is real. It is present. It permeates out of the very core of their beings.

The spiritual formation of your forged family will rely on the presence of God, not on the idea of him.

My wife, Maddie, and I regularly host prayer experiences with college students. They come to life in settings where they are allowed to believe that God is actually alive and moving. Watching university students pray for each other makes my heart explode because I know that God uses their childlike faith to usher in bold moves of his kingdom.

We hosted one prayer meeting that happened to be in an open field. Students walked around the large open space, laid hands on one another, and prayed their guts out together.

An eighteen-year-old reminisced about that time with me the following week:

> I was prayed for. I cannot remember what was prayed, or what was said. But I do know this. I felt the Father's love for the first time. I felt the love of God fill me from the inside out. God said over and over, "I love you. You are my son."
>
> I drove home while weeping. And when I got home, I kept weeping. The tangible love of God rested within me, and I cried in his presence for hours. Before that night, I would have said that the gospel is for other people. That God's love is good, but it is for others. I could not believe that it is actually for me. But in that moment of prayer, for the very first time, I knew that the gospel was for me too. God loves even me.

God's manifest presence moves faith from the head to the heart. The Holy Spirit borrows information from our minds and then uses it to illuminate our spirits. The problem is that the Holy Spirit wants us to worship him with our whole person, yet online church is categorically disembodied. The Spirit needs our mind, spirit, and body to form us into the love of God. First Corinthians 6:13 says it well: "The body is . . . meant . . . for the Lord, and the Lord for the body." We are his, our physical selves included.

Forged families will experience the love of God together. There is a lot that binds them: age, struggle, friendship, etc. But their tightest bond is fused in a shared pursuit of God. Forged families grow into the love of God as a community. They will learn to receive love from God and to love God as they worship together in person.

The Presence of Others

As the previous section focused on our embodied need of the presence of God, it only seems right that this section now focuses on our embodied need of the presence of others. All we need to do is look at the second greatest commandment in Scripture. The first is to love God with all your heart, and with all your soul, and with all your strength, and with all your mind (Matt. 22:37; Deut. 6:5). And the silver-medal commandment follows: "love your neighbor as yourself" (Matt. 22:39).

The call to Christian discipleship is not just to love God in every way, but to love your neighbor wholeheartedly as well. Loving God and loving others are attached at the hip. We know who God is, but who is your neighbor? Dallas Willard says that anyone can be your neighbor. The more relevant question is: To whom will you be a neighbor? Meaning, who will you choose to love?[5] For Jesus, our neighbors are the people we choose to love.

Many world religions have some form of this commandment. Buddhism's goes like this: *hurt not others in a way that you would find hurtful.* C. S. Lewis was quick to point out the advancement of that commandment within Christianity: love your neighbor as yourself. Followers of Jesus are asked not just to avoid hurting others, but to actively love and serve them. That means that forged families will be a community of neighbors, people looking to serve and love one another.

Building a community of twenty-somethings who make good on the previous statement is easier said than done. However difficult, love will be the dominant characteristic of any group that carries the name *family* with integrity. You must give emerging adults a training ground in love if they are to be spiritually formed. What better way of doing that than by serving others in their forged family?

My doorbell rang. My friend Eric was standing at the threshold of my house with a toolbox and his one-year-old son who ran betwixt his legs. I said hello and asked him: "What are you doing here?" He was an unexpected guest.

"I'm here to fix your toilet."

My toilet had broken earlier that day. I had texted Eric to see if he knew of any plumbers in town that he would recommend. He never responded to my text. Instead, he chose to arrive after work with his tool set.

Eric came in and got to work. I sat in my living room and listened to the clanks and buzz of power tools. It was the sound of a true handyman's project. About half an hour later, the job was finished. My toilet flushed voraciously, and Eric went on his way.

Eric is in my band that meets every week for encouragement, discernment, confession, and prayer. This is the most tightly bonded forged family that I have ever been a part of. We really do operate like family. Serving one another like that is natural. Our band is the epicenter of neighboring in the way of Jesus. It is the first group that we look to serve and love.

We do not wait to be asked for help. We step in to meet a need when we realize it exists within our forged family. This is to *love your neighbor as yourself.* Your emerging adults want friends like this. They long to be cared for in intimate ways, and to care for others. Interdependency is key to building a tight-knit community. This mode of living is entirely countercultural. We live in a day of isolation and internet connection. Friendships hosted online provide little to no opportunity for love and service. If the next move of God is to be a revolution of love, then it will be a movement hosted in person.

The difference between the manifest presence of God and the omnipresence of God is the same difference between being in the room with a close friend or just receiving a text message from them. We might know their love in concept, but true love is felt when we are served by others. There is a distinction between online and in-person relationships that registers emotionally and spiritually within us. The ministry of presence takes us beyond communication and into communion. Forged families spend time together, listen to each other, and serve one another.

Young adults come to life when they are given the opportunity to serve and love their friends in practical ways. Their stage of life is a prime time for discovering personal gifting. They are in a constant process of exploring their calling and gifting. People in their twenties are constantly asking: Who am I? How do I fulfill my purpose in the world? Your forged family can play a role in helping them answer those questions because *young adults will discover their spiritual gifting when they serve.* The spiritual gifts will be ignited when they put faith in action. They need spaces to serve others and to love them. It is very practical when you think about it. The spiritual gift of administration will never be discovered if they are never asked to organize. A teaching gift will not be discovered if they're not asked to teach. A healing gift will not be discovered if they are never challenged to pray for the sick.

But, when young adults are invited into a community where they are asked to give themselves in love and service, then the Holy Spirit will supernaturally activate gifting within them. If asked to intercede, they might discover a prophetic gifting. When asked to serve the marginalized, they might uncover a gift of mercy. A person in their twenties will discover that they hold a charismatic gift if they are invited into a forged family where neighborly love is a natural occurrence. This works both to grow them in their love for others and for the good of the community (1 Peter 4:10).[6]

Loving your neighbor as yourself will be impossible in a community that exists solely online. Emerging adults need to be in the presence of others before this will happen. They are hungry for community that provides the kind of intimate love that can only happen around the dinner table. They long for friends to show up unannounced on their doorstep, to be on kingdom mission with people who are like-hearted, to serve and give themselves wholly to meaningful projects, and to love their friends deeply.

If you can build interdependent communities for people in this stage of life, then a generation will come alive in spiritual gifting and identity in God. Family-like community is a powerful tool for embedding people in their faith. It is a nourishing soil that will help young adults grow deep roots in God.

The silver-medal commandment requires full-bodied discipleship, something that online ministry cannot provide in and of itself.

Spring of 2020

Deep discipleship and spiritual formation still happen primarily through in-person gatherings. Emerging generations are transformed by the presence of God and the presence of each other. It's not that online communication is not of value; it is of value. But group gatherings still matter for our world and for emerging adults. Their lives are changed when they share the same space. This was no more evident at any time in my life than with the Black Lives Matter (BLM) movement of 2020.

The death of Breonna Taylor hit hard in my area. I was scrolling through Twitter the first time I laid eyes on the story. I could not believe that such an unspeakable tragedy occurred so close to my home. I was embarrassed, shocked, and horrified that her death was largely overlooked by people in our state. It took months after her death, and a national news publication, to expose what had happened to Breonna. A substantial cry for justice did end up taking place, but only after the story went viral.

The BLM movement swept the nation in spring of 2020 after the George Floyd video went viral. The sounds and images of his death brought to light the reality of racial injustice in our society and prodded concerned and angry citizens into the streets. More than fifteen million people chanted George and Breonna's names as they marched for social justice in the following couple months, making BLM one of the largest movements in American history.[7]

Time magazine called it the "The Overdue Awakening."[8] The movement transformed how people think on a widespread scale and then mobilized them to campaign for change. I had the privilege of marching alongside African American pastors in my city as part of a statewide push to make Breonna's story the last of its kind. Although the efforts received marginal success with Breonna's Law being passed in the city of Louisville, Kentucky, there is still much work to be done.

Spring of 2020 is an important time to reflect on for a number of reasons. One reason is that it gives an example of how digital life and our physical world interact. Online communication was important for the BLM movement. The internet is the most powerful tool of communication in human history and its power was felt during that period. Websites, email, and social media spurred people into action. But the moment would not have been called by some to be the largest in American history without the in-person rallies.

Without physical rallies, the deaths of George and Breonna may have been a speed bump on the road to the next viral moment. The masses made their frustration, anger, and disappointment felt because they brought what was communicated online into the real world. Their pain was embodied and taken into the streets. The marches ensured that George and Breonna's deaths, along with the deaths of many others, would not be easily forgotten. Digital communication might provide necessary support for a movement in today's world, but it is not an adequate host for one.

We are not yet past the time when in-person gatherings matter. Our lives and the world change through our real, embodied interactions with one another.

Digital Ministry without Compromise

Christian leaders tried to transition their communities online in a hurry once quarantine hit. The spring of 2020 brought an absolute gold rush of churches who tried to own the digital space. Some people already had seamless online experiences and claimed squatter's rights to online church. Others redirected their entire ministries in an attempt to become *the church of the internet*. And others simply went through the motion of recording worship and posting it as a stopgap, hoping things would quickly go back to normal.

The temptation in our day is to measure our leadership success in virality. But the reality is that only a select few Christian leaders will ever have viral impact. The top .01 percent of Christian communicators will own the digital world and the rest of us will have to measure our impact in other ways.

Even now, I am constantly approached by people in my own house church movement who tell me of the sermons from other pastors that they listen to online. Weekly, I hear about the sermons from pastors in places like New York, Los Angeles, London, Hong Kong, and Australia. And guess what? I listen to and watch many of those pastors as well. That's okay. I am not upset about it or offended by it. Widely watched preaching and teaching is a service to the big-C church.

But virality is not the future of Christian leadership. Only those with transcendent communication skills will be able to cut their chops online. The rest of us will make important and lasting impacts in other ways. God has a plan for the future of the local church and local Christian leader.

That's why I believe the next wave of pastors who lead the church into the future will do so by developing localized discipleship networks. Young Christians already have instant access to an inexhaustible library of top-level resources, sermons, teaching, etc. But what they do not have is friendship. What they do not have are spiritual parents. What they do not have are communities of people whom they love deeply and who love them in return.

Online communication is good for sharing information, but it is not good for the transformation of the heart. If you want to make a lasting impact in the lives of Millennials and Gen Zers, then give them a listening ear. Give them access to your life where you model the teachings and life of Jesus. Give them a community of people who love and serve one another and share kingdom mission in their city.

Give them a forged family. You may never go viral, but your leadership in their lives is invaluable. They might consume five online sermons a week, but those will likely be forgotten. Those words will flutter in one ear and out the other. What emerging adults will remember—the words that will sink deep in their hearts for weeks, months, and years to come—are the words spoken to them around your dinner table.

They will remember the times they confessed to friends, the times when they received prayer for healing, and the times when a listening ear was given to them in their hour of need. Viral content will play a role in the future of the church, but the formational power and relevance of the church for emerging adult Christians will be found within forged families.

Do not only give young adults information about God and the Christian life. Build a community that lives out those habits and instructions. Family-like communities transmit lifestyle. What you disciple some into, others will catch. Through a forged family, the life you model has the potential to ripple down through the generations.

George Whitefield and John Wesley were perhaps the two most recognizable leaders in the Second Great Awakening. Both were prolific preachers who spoke to tens of thousands, but Whitefield, by most accounts, was the better communicator of the two. He has long been remembered for his commanding presence, his booming voice, and his persuasive language.[9] Yet, when talking about his ministry in comparison to Wesley's he said, "My brother Wesley acted wisely. The souls that were awakened under his ministry he joined in societies, and thus preserved the fruit of his labor. This I neglected, and my people are a rope of sand."

Wesley went through the trouble of organizing his followers in *societies* or *bands*. These were small groups of people who got messy in each other's lives by vulnerably and bravely encouraging each other in the way of Jesus. They met regularly, confessed their hidden sin, discussed Scripture, and discerned God's direction together. Wesley assembled his converts into what is essentially a forged family.

Whitefield did no such thing. Today there are millions of Wesleyans roaming the planet, but no discernible spiritual descendants of Whitefield, despite his superior teaching gift. Whitefield himself called his converts a *rope of sand*, easily lost between his fingers.

Virality is not the future of church leadership. The deeper impact on emerging generations will be had by men and women who bother to intimately disciple young Christians and who develop forged families that journey together in the Christian life.

Digital communication is important, but for most of us, it is best used to support our embodied discipleship communities. It is a tool that can help us build the local forged family that emerging adults truly need. Digital communication should be a means to an end, not an end in itself.

CHAPTER EIGHT

Band Together
168 Community

You can trust us to stick to you through thick and
thin—to the bitter end. And you can trust us to
keep any secret of yours—closer than you your-
self keep it. But you cannot trust us to let you face
trouble alone. . . . We are your friends, Frodo.
—Merry Brandybuck, *The Fellowship of the Ring*, J. R. R. Tolkien[1]

GEN ZERS AND MILLENNIALS DO NOT INTUITIVELY
understand how to build tight-knit community. It would not
be lacking in our churches or in their generations if this kind
of fellowship were a natural part of their culture. Depression,
anxiety, and loneliness instead tell their tale. Emerging adults
desperately long to be known, yet many do not have the space or
the skills to build friendships on their own.

We have used a lot of words throughout this book to the
describe intimate young adult communities. We've called it
tight-knit, non-casual, family-like, etc. But what does that really
mean? How do we begin building a community that bonds people
together? What are the concrete qualities and nature of the relationships that we are talking about? How can we help emerging

generations break through superficial-level relationships and develop soul-level friendships?

Start by taking advantage of the opportunities provided in that stage of life. Most twenty-somethings are going through some kind of transition at any given moment. They are most likely confused about their future and are discerning where they want to go in life. Their searching delves beneath the surface-level and unearths a deeply personal quest within each of them to form an identity and discover a calling.

Young adults want to explore the depths of who they are and their future to come with others. This makes them uniquely open to soul-level friendships in this stage of life. They are hungry for them, but do not know how to acquire them. This is where you step in. Your forged family can be a relationship training ground. You have the ability to model spiritual friendship and to teach them how to invest in relationships that will last a lifetime.

In this chapter we will show you how to capitalize on the opportunities in emerging adulthood for community building. Their big life-stage questions can lead them to spiritual friendship. Your forged family can provide the soil for trusting, vulnerable, and long-lasting relationships. Teach them to band together, and a *tight-knit, non-casual, family-like* community will emerge.

Too Many Coffee Options

Have you ever gone to the grocery store for one item, only to leave holding five or more items an hour later? This happens to me every once in a while. I'll walk into the store with a specific purchase in mind and then struggle to choose which brand I want to buy. I find myself staring down a vast array of brand options— while elderly women buzz by me pushing carts like pro NASCAR drivers—until I leave frustrated, with a product selection that I'm neither happy with nor confident in!

I am frequently paralyzed in the coffee aisle. You must understand my love for coffee before you understand my frustration when purchasing it. Morning coffee is nothing short of a sacred ritual for me. Every sunrise I'll wander over to the coffee cabinet (yes, I have a cabinet reserved for coffee) to grab my Chemex pour-over. I'll bust out the coffee beans, grind them, heat the water to 201°F, add it to 400g of grinds, and voilà! Coffee appears and livens up my morning prayer. This alchemy is both scientific and spiritual; any change to the ingredients could prove disastrous to my coffee and, consequently, my prayer life. The brand of coffee I choose at the store is crucial. The selection cannot be made haphazardly or hastily.

I have my go-to coffee brands at the grocery store, but a real issue develops if my regular coffee is missing from the aisle. The problem is that there are a lot of factors to consider when making an in-the-moment decision. For instance, poor-quality coffee would be a sin against the morning ritual. But who has the cash flow required for a top-brand buy every time? I have to put my kids through college (my hypothetical kids, assuming the college bubble hasn't burst in twenty years) and simply cannot purchase premium bags on the regular. Also, whole bean coffee is a must. It's the only way to achieve a fresh coffee aroma every morning. That means that pre-ground coffee is not an option. And forget about artificially flavored beans; flavors like cinnamon dolce and French vanilla are beyond unnatural—they're criminal.

In summary, the purchase cannot be too expensive, too cheap, too fake, pre-ground, or unnatural. A misstep in any of these directions would ruin the next twenty cups of morning rituals. Thus, it is a little difficult to select a coffee bean from one of the literal fifty options. Sometimes I'll go to the store on a mission for coffee only to leave after thirty minutes of intense staring and calculating.

None of us is immune to this dilemma. It can happen with any person and with any product. The grocery store is full of hundreds of little decisions that will make a person insane. There are fifty types of coffee beans, forty frozen pizza labels, thirty brands of spaghetti sauce, twenty producers of nuts, and ten varieties of milk from which to choose. It's amazing that we have any leftover time in our lives after we've finished making these tedious (and often meaningless) dietary decisions.

The grocery store highlights what is true about the lives of emerging adults. They stand frozen in the face of major life decisions, overwhelmed by the options, and uncertain of how to make the choice that will move them forward. They exist in a world where personal freedom has exploded into every facet of life and the possibilities are endless. They are told that options equals freedom, and that freedom equals salvation. But in reality, the road of unlimited potential often ends with choice exhaustion and chronic anxiety. Mark Sayers wrote:

> The expansion of choice anxiety and information overload has created an endless sense of confusion and lostness, leading many to recoil from making any forward steps, in fear of making the wrong decision.[2]

A constant barrage of decisions can put a real strain on our emotional health and well-being. This is why entrepreneurs like Albert Einstein and Steve Jobs have been known to wear the same outfit every day (Einstein, the gray suit, and Jobs, the black shirt). Eliminating small decisions freed up their minds and emotions so they could tackle larger issues.[3] Emerging adults can learn this lesson from their example: we need to lighten our decision-making load.

More life-altering choices are made in young adulthood than in any other stage of life. Emerging adults find themselves wandering in the aisles of love, career, and community. They can feel paralyzed by the questions that constantly swirl in their minds: *Who will I marry? What career will I work? Where will I live?*

These meaning-making questions seem complicated because they shape our lives. However, breaking them into categories can help release emerging adults from their grasp. The major muddle of our early twenties can be boiled down to three simple categories: vocation, location, and spouse.

> **Vocation**: What am I going to do with my life?
> **Spouse**: Who am I going to spend my life with?
> **Location**: Where am I going to live?[4]

Dan, a twenty-one-year-old college student, had not been accepted into any of the dentistry schools to which he had applied. The final rejection letter came at the end of his senior spring semester. He had carried the hopes of becoming a dentist since freshman year, only to have his dreams dashed the month before graduation. He found himself at the end of his senior year without a plan. The rejection letter came in and Dan approached me the next day with some big questions: "Where am I supposed to live after college? What job and career am I supposed to pursue?"

I had a lot of sympathy for Dan. He had to face the humongous questions of his stage of life in a short period of time. But the reality is that everyone in their twenties wrestles through that same process of discernment. In a land of opportunity, the future can seem overwhelming and daunting. There are unlimited options, but young adults feel pressure to make the perfect decision. Many like Dan experience extreme anxiety around vocation, location, and spouse because these issues are so central to our identity. Emerging adults want friends who can help them make these big decisions in the grocery store of life.

What Is God's Will for My Life?

Dan did not only come to me with questions about his location and vocation. He came wanting to know: "Where was God in all of this confusion? Has God abandoned me? Did I miss the will of God for my life by not getting accepted to dentistry school?"

For emerging adult Christians there is another layer of question-asking. Underneath the anxiety about location, vocation, and spouse is the simple question: What is God's will for my life?

Ultimately, this is what Christians in their twenties are wondering. Everyone wants to know that there is a plan and purpose for their life; to know that they aren't adrift at sea, lost and alone. The meaning of life adds weight to the discernment process. Emerging adults fear making a wrong decision that will lead to them missing out on God's big plan for their life.

The tricky thing is that God's will is not primarily concerned with the concrete decisions one makes around location, vocation, and spouse.

That's not to say that God thinks those things are trivial; God very much cares about the directional decisions of our lives. But—as any quality pastor would note—God is primarily interested in who we are and not what we do.

He is more concerned with the content of our character and the quality of our love than he is with things like vocation, location, and spouse. Check out these verses from Scripture that all talk about God's will. I think you'll notice a theme.

- "For this is the will of God, your sanctification: that you abstain from sexual immorality." (1 Thess. 4:3)
- "Give thanks in all circumstances; for this is the will of God in Christ Jesus for you." (1 Thess. 5:18)
- "For this is the will of God, that by doing good you should put to silence the ignorance of foolish people." (1 Peter 2:15)
- "Therefore do not be foolish, but understand what the will of the Lord is. And do not get drunk with wine, for that is debauchery, but be filled with the Spirit." (Eph. 5:17–18)
- "He has told you, O man, what is good; and what does the Lord require of you but to do justice, and to love kindness, and to walk humbly with your God?" (Micah 6:8)

What is the one thing that all these verses have in common? They highlight the fact that God's will has more to do with our character than our life decisions! Our main calling is to Jesus, to grow into his likeness.

> The Christian journey, therefore, is an intentional and continual commitment to a lifelong process of growth toward wholeness in Christ. It is a process of "growing up in every way into him who is the head, into Christ" (Eph. 4:15), until we "attain to . . . mature personhood, to the measure of the stature of the fullness of Christ" (Eph. 4:13). It is for this purpose that God is present and active in every moment of our lives.[5]

Discernment and holiness are intertwined. They are part and parcel with emerging adults discovering who they are to become. *You have to work out character if you're going to work out where God is leading you in other areas of life.*

Twenty-somethings want to know that God is with them as they navigate their journey. They exist in a hotbed of character and identity formation that makes them open to help from friends and community.

Your forged family is the perfect place for young adults to work out calling and holiness. The decisions they face are disorienting. They live in choice anxiety, overwhelmed by the stress of discerning a future. Friends are needed to help them sort it all out.

You can help them meet their largest felt needs while also giving them space to bond together in a journey toward Christlikeness. Forged families are the perfect place to discover answers to life's biggest questions. Give them the opportunity, and they will vulnerably explore the depths of God's will with others. Banding is one tool you can use to help them build deep and intimate friendships in this quest.

God's Remedy for Woundedness

I have banded together with a group of young men for the past few years. We gather weekly to meet as brothers to pray, to discern God's presence, and to pursue holiness. We sit on the stoop for a couple hours each week and share life.

We mostly just talk and pray. Banding provides a space to confess sin and help each other discern where God is leading in our lives. Most of the time it is pretty unspectacular, just ordinary conversation.

But sometimes, it's miraculous. I've seen God use this little band of relationships to save marriages, provide financially, and physically heal the sick. We know one another intimately and encourage each other toward God. We support each other and love each other.

We have entered into deep and intimate friendship. It is rare for a group of men in their mid-twenties and mid-thirties to have those kinds of relationships. Our bond is special. Our band is family.

We can expect a twenty-first-century renewal in the American church to be marked by this kind of family-like community. This, of course, would not be a completely novel movement as far as historical church revivals are concerned. When God moves and changes people's hearts, new believers tend to gather with others who will encourage them to live out of their new identity. The Methodist awakening of the eighteenth century (as one example) was carried out by small groups of men and women who banded together to pursue God with one another.

Wesley bands were small groups of Christians who met together to actively grow in their faith. Their goal was to experience a transformation into holiness and to become the people of faith that God desired. They met regularly, but not around a theological subject or book.

They gathered around confession and discernment. People were bonded together in the common goal to move into Christlikeness and to pursue the will of God in their lives. Wesley bands shared vulnerably and openly. They stewarded deeply intimate relationships. They were real, raw, and honest. Just look at the questions they answered together:

1. What known sins have you committed since our last meeting?
2. What temptations have you met with?
3. How were you delivered?
4. What have you thought, said, or done of which you doubt whether it be sin or not?
5. Have nothing you desire to keep secret?[6]

Do you have anything you desire to keep secret is an insane question to ask of another person. It is an even more insane question to answer. Wesley band meetings for the early Methodists were hard-hitting and intensely personal. They allowed for people to know each other deeply and to be deeply known.

Have life discussions at this level of vulnerability, and you will see the Holy Spirit work radically in your life. Banding spurs on growth and encourages change from the inside out.

I was once in a college men's group where we were challenged to answer several questions and to discuss them in triads. The group had been together for a couple months, but this was the first time that we intentionally talked together. We started by taking some alone time to look at and pray over the questions.

A junior named Eric raised his hand to share with the group when we came back together. He chose to discuss the question: "What is one thing you wish to keep secret?" This is a dangerous question to ask, and an even more dangerous question to answer!

Tears welled up in his eyes as he began to share about a car wreck that had altered his father's life. The accident occurred when Eric was in the third grade. He was shocked at the time of the wreck. His father survived the crash, but a couple of facts surrounding that day have altered Eric's relationship with him ever since.

They discovered alcohol in his dad's system at the time of the crash. And to make matters worse, Eric's mom discovered that his dad had been adulterous. She found texts during his recovery that proved he was having an affair in the months leading up to his accident.

The wreck caused permanent damage to their marriage and to his dad's health. He sustained a brain injury in the accident that has altered his thinking forever. Eric hated his father for being an addict and an adulterer, but kept his feelings secret. The accident left his dad mentally ill. He did not remember the accident or his previous life. Eric was never able to confront him about the hurt he inflicted on him or his family. Eric was left for years to deal with his pain unresolved and on his own.

Eric cried while sharing the story. He said that he had never talked openly about it before. He had grown up in a home with a father he resented, but he couldn't resolve this frustration because his dad's brain wasn't the same after the accident. Eric kept this frustration and resentment packed inside himself for years. He never brought it up with friends before because he was so terribly embarrassed by the truth. He felt destined to be like his father, to live a life of addiction and adultery. These lies buried themselves deep in his heart and attached themselves to his identity.

Eric shared this for the first time with our group and we could all sense how monumental of a moment this was for him. We got to encourage him, speak truth to him about his life, and pray over him. Eric is a weight lifter and a macho man, but chose to step into vulnerability that night. It took bravery to open the door for healing. He mentioned afterward that a huge weight had been lifted off his shoulders. Eric felt free from burden after years of being exhausted by its weight. Our small group has continued to walk with him as friends. We have helped him heal and discern his life's direction.

God uses banding to take down the strongholds in our lives. It allows for deep wounds, sin, and lies to be heard, forgiven, and dismantled. Eric's story is just one example from many bands I've been around that have answered these penetrating questions.

I have seen people in bands confess serious sexual sin or dark insecurities and admit to all kinds of personal failure. These moments are the first steps into freedom, holiness, and the will of God. It is amazing to see Christians rally around one another to steward the presence of God in each other's lives. Confessions and moments of vulnerability are often met with forgiveness, compassion, and tearful prayer.

Banding does not just give space for healing; it lays the groundwork for shared discernment. I've witnessed bands help each other discern life calls, romantic relationships, and career choices. Banding relationships address a felt need in people that are paralyzed by choice anxiety. Friends who share these conversations are going to have a complete picture of one another's lives and can help each other discern where God is and where he is leading. These groups become much-needed help in the grocery store aisle of life.

Through banding, your church can guide young adults into holiness while also helping them navigate the questions of location, vocation, and spouse. The life transformation they desire is made possible through the Holy Spirit and trusted relationships.

These generations are characteristically shallow in their spiritual conversations. Most don't have any discussions at all about spiritual life with their peers or even with their significant others. This certainly contributes to them feeling frozen in the grocery store of life. They have a desperate felt need for people with whom they can band together and walk through decision-making alongside—whether they realize it or not. This is where the church can step in and help.

Of course, banding—which, in many ways, is just a designated space for deep spiritual friendship—requires much more than a regular space for talking. Forged families will create space for spiritual friendship in one form or another. But intimate relationships require vulnerability and trust. Confession and healing will not happen without intentional cultivation of deep friendship.

168 Community

Emerging adults are slow to trust others. They are afraid of how others might judge them if they shared their true selves. We all feel this way to a certain extent. It is hard to share our inner lives with anyone else. The fear of rejection blocks us from spiritual friendship.

Our society affirms feeling as truth. In this framework, any feeling is something that must be lived out to achieve an authentic life. Every action that is true to one's own emotions is a right action. The only sin is to not live out your true inner self.

Postmodern society upholds the journey of salvation as one of self-actualization. You are liberated when your inner feelings come out. This is different from the Christian journey of salvation, which is one of inner transformation. Christians believe that Jesus asks us at times to put aside our feelings and desires so that we might live into Jesus' vision of human flourishing.

Christian discipleship is an ongoing commitment of self-denial for the sake of following the way of Jesus. We take on his identity by trusting his teaching and modeling our lives after his example. The thought of bringing others into this journey with us is incredibly scary for young adults. It gives others access to our successes and our struggles. What if they think that our emotions, feelings, or actions are wrong?

Our banded friends might encourage us not to act on our desires and to change the way we think or believe. The idea that we would allow them to hold us accountable to the standard of Jesus is culturally insane and very scary.

Emerging adults will not simply trust anyone with their inner lives. It opens them up for far too much judgment and harm. Only trusted friends with whom they are deeply committed will ever have this privilege. There must be a security within the friendship where each person knows that the other loves them and has their best interest in mind.

A once-a-week accountability group will not be sufficient to build this kind of community. Trust will not be built through a weekly conversation. Deep levels of vulnerability will require shared lives between friends who see each other throughout the week. Friends with whom you confess to will be friends that you share other parts of your life with as well. James 5:16 says: "Therefore, confess your sins to one another and pray for one another, that you may be healed. The prayer of a righteous person has great power as it is working." This command to confess was given to the family-like community of the early church. Those who have sinned haven't just sinned against God, but against one another as well. James 5:16 came at a section's end where James pleads for others to not grumble, complain, or argue within Christian community.

It came on the heels of James urging the sick in the community to have the elders pray over them for healing. Elders get involved when necessary to straighten things out. Why? Because the entire community is affected by one person's sin—by one person's grumbling, arguing, or gossiping. The first-century church worked out the kinks of sin dysfunction in the house church context. Good luck hiding the stench of sin in that kind community!

Forged families will be made up of people who see each other in everyday life. I have heard it said that it takes two hundred face-to-face hours before someone is considered a *best friend*. That's a lot of face time! Shared space and shared experiences are the only ways to build the kind of trust necessary for intimate spiritual friendships.

Tight-knit, non-casual, family-like Christian communities are communities of confession and discernment where young adults have conversations that break below the shallow everyday norm and where they confess to one another, pray, and discern God's direction for each other's lives. This takes a massive amount of trust—the kind of trust that is only built through a lot of shared life.

I lived with the people that I also worked alongside for my first five years in ministry. We banded together every week to practice accountability, discernment, and prayer. These weekly times shaped me through my early twenties. However formative these hour-long meetings were, they paled in comparison to the way those relationships molded me in the other 167 hours of the week.

I lived with the men who were in my band. We shared meals, movies, vacations, and nights out. We also lived on mission together. There were plenty of late nights where we stayed up praying and worshipping. We discipled younger men together and contended for the kingdom of God to be formed in our city. Banded relationships will not happen if we only give them our attention in a weekly meeting. But deep spiritual friendships will form if we build them throughout all 168 hours of our week.

A Matter of Belonging, Not Attending

A Christian community that offers banding—family-like communities of confession, forgiveness, and commitment—will be practically irresistible to emerging generations. What could possibly be more attractive than friends who could help you answer the questions of location, vocation, and spouse, while also helping you discern God's will for your life?

The tricky thing is that this kind of community doesn't happen as a result of casual church attendance. We will never meet the needs of the generations or the needs of our church communities if we're asking the question: What in our church can emerging adults attend?

Banded communities cannot form within that environment and mindset. We must depart from attendance to ask the better questions: Where in our community can emerging adults belong? How can we build trusted friendship among young adults? What can we do to create space for intentional spiritual conversation? Banding is a matter of belonging, not attending.

The emerging adult's search for a life purpose and God's will could lead them into Christian community. But only if we offer them forged families in which they can belong.

A young adult that finds belonging—spiritual friendship and banded discipleship—will see their future with clarity. They will not only discover their own destinies, but will walk into holiness along the way. Oh, and with banded relationships, they just might remain committed to your Christian community through their twenties.

CHAPTER NINE

Serve Together

Training Warriors in Their Twice-Given Gifts

> *True joy, happiness, and inner peace comes*
> *from the giving of ourselves to others.*
> —Henri Nouwen, *Life of the Beloved*[1]

I RECENTLY LED A PRAYER TIME FOR A GROUP OF PEOPLE near my house. Afterward, a forty-five-year-old man approached me to say that it was his first time ever praying out loud with someone. "Oh, are you new to the faith?" I asked.

"Well . . . no . . . I've attended church my whole life."

I needed a stool, something to sit down on. A Christian man, in his forties, had never before prayed out loud with other Christians. The shock of hearing those words almost knocked me to the ground. This is the most basic of all Christian spiritual practices. Prayer is, point-blank, the only way to talk to God. And he had never exercised it before with others? How could he be expected to grow in his faith if he's not learning to pray alongside fellow believers?

The prayer exercise revealed some big problems. This lifelong churchgoer could not disciple another person because he himself had never been taught or modeled Jesus' most basic habits. But the problem doesn't lie in this man's heart; he was willing to pray when the opportunity was offered. The problem lies within our systems.

Many people can walk through church doors week-in and week-out for a lifetime, without being asked to practice the lifestyle of Jesus with others. It reveals that too much emphasis is on the Sunday-morning teaching for a believer's development. American Christianity feels spiritually stale and there's no wonder why. If someone is never challenged to practice the spiritual disciplines within the church, then they are unlikely to take the kingdom to the world.

Now, imagine being a war general. You've prepared your troops with a lot of . . . lectures. You've drawn up battle stances, outlined regiment formations, and explained hand-to-hand combat. And now, after hours of lecturing and listening, it's time to go to battle. How do we imagine our army of well-intentioned warriors will perform?

There has not been any experience, nor hands-on training, nor any embodied practicing; only observance and listening. No one but the teachers have any leadership experience. No one is accustomed to taking initiative. Our warriors are out of shape. My guess is that we'll lose the battle. In the words of philosopher Mike Tyson: "Everyone has a plan till they get punched in the face."

Yet, this is how many churches operate. They bring the potential troops in every week for a lecture. Their heart rate might go up. Their ears might be tickled. The contours of the spiritual life might be outlined for them. They might be inspired. But they are never asked to engage; never challenged to exercise; never given the opportunity to lead.

So they remain stagnant.

Spiritually comatose.

Inert.

It's not that they're not ready for battle. They've not even being trained. Many churches have—albeit unintentionally—cultivated observers, not participants; attendees, not disciples.

It's no wonder why so many leaders feel alone in the mission of the church, why ministry efforts can feel so lifeless, why growth is stunted, and why Christian adults remain spiritual children. Churches have an army at their disposal, waiting to be utilized. But they have been sidelined as passive observers. It makes you think: If emerging adults are allowed to float in and out of church without offering up so much as a prayer with others, then how many of their spiritual gifts lie dormant, waiting to be activated?

Twenty-somethings are full of fire and passion. They aspire to be world-changers and global leaders. Many of them have unbridled optimism in the potential for good. Their early years of adulthood are a time when they are exploring an emboldened relationship with God.

Those saints who walk through the transition from high school to college with Jesus are full of faith. And they are curious. These young adults want to discover the endless wonders of God. They are asking: "Does the God that I read about in Scripture inhabit my everyday life?"

They want to go on faith adventurers alongside a present, powerful, and loving God. Emerging adults are willing to try bold prayer, to risk in evangelism, or to explore the gifting of the Holy Spirit. These trailblazers are flexible, fluid, and passionate. They want to test the limits of faith and are not afraid of getting scuffed up a bit in the process.

But time and again, I hear these phrases from college students across the country:

Pray for me, Austin. I do not feel like I belong in my church.
There is no place for me to serve or lead.
My opinions are unwanted and unheard.
I do not know anyone at my church.
I feel alone in my spiritual walk.

Young adults are full of passion for God, but feel uninvited to serve or lead within the church.

Church leaders find themselves on the other side of this coin. From the leader's perspective, the younger generations are unwilling to commit or serve. Many are afraid to ask much of the emerging adults within their community because they might scare them away or come off as too demanding. So twenty-somethings remain unchallenged observers of worship.

The warriors in the Sunday seats feel unwanted and church leaders do not know how to call them into action.

This is where you step in. Emerging adults have found belonging in your forged family. Ask them to be involved in the everyday life of your community. Do not be afraid of breeching their comfort zone. The loving relationships within the community give you a safe place to challenge them. And the truth is that most young adult Christians want to be stretched. They are hungry to practice a real faith and will risk to do so.

This chapter will show you that emerging adults are actually the perfect people to challenge. They desire to live an active faith, making it easy for you to invite them into deep levels of sacrifice, service, and action.

You can help to move young adults from observation to participation within the church. But be warned: the army in the seats will not be activated by top-down leadership that asks them to do menial tasks. Asking them to be a greeter twice a month will not satisfy their desire for involvement. Emerging generations will not participate if that participation begins and ends with setting up a Sunday-morning experience.

Young adults will be activated into kingdom contribution if we treat our Christian communities as training facilities. Relying on a Sunday message to equip them for church contribution will fail. They need community and relational hands-on experience to sort out the practices of faith. Bring them into a community that shows them what a living faith looks like, and you will watch them come to life in their gifting. They will discover what God has given them to contribute to the church and will be willing to commit, lead, and serve within your community.

You see, these warriors actually want to get dirty in the trenches. They want to be on the front lines of risk-taking and are not afraid of some hands-on combat. Teach them to pray, care for the poor, share their faith, and move in the power of the Holy Spirit, and these warriors will be released into battle.

The Dojo

Every morning my friend Larry drives to a massive Toyota plant with thousands of workers. He walks through the large facility, passing by all the machines and workers building cars that day. Having walked through the larger work facility, he arrives at a special area set aside for training new employees.

This set-aside training area is split into two sections: a classroom and a miniature version of the larger plant. Larry oversees orientation and apprenticing for these new employees. He takes the new hires into the classroom where they are instructed. Then, he takes them into the miniature version of the plant where they practice all the work they will one day need to perform out in the larger plant. Larry works alongside them, helping them to perfect their craft before making it out to the assembly line.

Toyota does not just rely on teaching or hands-on experience to train their hires. Rather, new employees learn through a trial-and-error process alongside a skilled expert like Larry. He knows how to perform the needed skill and is there to assist them through a trial-and-error learning process.

I love the name that Toyota has given their training facility. They call it The Dojo. The word is usually reserved for the Japanese fighting style of karate. A dojo is a hall or establishment where apprentice students come to learn the martial art of karate from a master sensei. But in a dojo, karate is not simply a matter of learning the mechanics of fighting.

It is in the dojo where students learn the philosophy, actions, and lifestyle of karate, and they do this in relationship with someone who can help them through a hands-on trial-and-error process. They are also surrounded by a community of other students who are also testing out newfound skills and practices within the context of a community.

The word *dojo* means "the way" in English. Students learn the way of karate from a sensei. Larry trains his employees in "the way" of a Toyota worker. And the emerging adults in your forged family can learn to live in "the way of Jesus." None of these ways can rely solely on verbal teaching or instruction. They all must include hands-on learning experiences with an equipped leader and within a trusted community.[2]

The early church believers were known as followers of the way of Jesus. Much has been made in this book of the Acts 2:42–47 vision of the early church. We do not need to rehash all that has previously been said in this moment. But it is worth pointing out that the apostles gathered the new converts at Pentecost into family-like communities that centered their lives around the teachings and practices of Jesus. The new converts were put into dojos, where they learned through practical experience how to live like Jesus lived and how to do what Jesus taught.

I planted Arise Church during the COVID pandemic of 2020. Arise is a movement of house churches that operates as one body in our city. We modeled our gatherings after the Acts 2:42 (NIV) verse: "They devoted themselves to the apostles' teaching and fellowship, to the breaking of bread and to prayer." Every Sunday our house churches gather in homes to eat a meal, sing, pray, and discuss Scripture and teaching. It is a not-so-subtle attempt to carbon-copy the gatherings and rhythms of the Acts 2 community.

These house churches usually have ten to fifteen people who attend. That means everyone intercedes when it is time for prayer, everyone sings when it is time for worship, and everyone discusses and reflects together on Scripture and teaching. It is intimate and intimidating at first (and a little awkward if some people choose to come and not participate!) but we are watching people come alive in their new gifting.

Some are learning to pray for the first time. Others are learning to interpret Scripture and apply it to their lives. And others are discovering that they have gifting in things like pastoral care, prophetic words, teaching, evangelism, social justice, worship leading, hospitality, and the like. We are watching people come alive in the gifts that they have to contribute to the church and the world because they are given a safe space to try new things and to get dirty in practicing the spiritual rhythms together.

I am not a house church purist. It is not the only legitimate way to do church, nor is this book an attempt to sell house church. But our house churches have provided spaces for many twenty-somethings to participate in worship, and their gifting has been unearthed along the way.

Any forged family can work as a Jesus dojo for emerging adults. You need not have a house church to provide space of participation and equipping. Training occurs anywhere that young believers gather for things like prayer or singing, Scripture and discussion, neighborhood engagement, or meals. Your forged family can invite young adults to participate in the lifestyle of Jesus and in the life of the church. As a sensei, you will teach and train. You are there to provide encouragement in failure and celebration in success. Your forged family is the perfect place for twenty-somethings to discover the spiritual gifts God has given to them.

The Pressure to Be Lebron

A person's early twenties is the middle school of adulthood. There's not an overwhelming amount of self-awareness, and identity-uncertainty flares up with this key question: What am I good at?

Emerging adults want to explore faith limits but will need some help in the journey of both self-discovery and God-discovery. Think about yourself at twenty years old. Did you know for certain what career you were going to work? Were you aware of the skills you would rely on to make it in the adult world? What about your kingdom contribution? Could you have confidently named your spiritual gifts at that age?

The answer to these questions—if you were anything like me—is probably *no*. Most young adults are excited to contribute, but are unsure what that actually looks like! That's why church-as-dojo is so important for them in this stage. They need a gym to wrestle through all the possibilities in practical ways. Only then will they discover their talents, traits, and unique contributions for the kingdom.

Discovering gifting is a key part of forming an identity in adulthood. Deep down, everyone wants to believe they've been given a one-of-a-kind skill that can bless the world. There is a reason we label these as *God-given abilities*. We watch Lebron James block a basketball shot and think, *What an amazing God-given ability! I wish I had skill like that!*

But most young adults are not child prodigies. They are insecure about their gifts. They see leaders on stage or within their community that seem otherworldly in their talent, and it leaves them wondering what they even have to offer. Communities that form these potential warriors will leave professionalism at the door of the training facility.

Our communities are not made of people with otherworldly talents. They are made of up people whose regular talents are blessed by God for the sake of the world. If given the chance, each young adult will discover they have a skill or gift to contribute to the church.

The classic spiritual gifts passage in Corinthians says it well:

> Now there are varieties of gifts, but the same Spirit; and there are varieties of service, but the same Lord; and there are varieties of activities, but it is the same God who empowers them all in everyone. *To each is given the manifestation of the Spirit for the common good.* (1 Cor. 12:4–7, emphasis added)

"To each is given" is an amazing little phrase that jumps out of this passage of Scripture. It implies that everyone has something to offer. The very thought that someone might go without a gift at Christmas makes us all sad. This is the kind of fear that sets in if we see others excelling in their spiritual gifts while we feel useless in the kingdom.

Many young adults look around at the spiritual giants in the church and wonder how they could ever impact the world in that way. We have good news to alleviate that anxiety: the Christmas tree is always full! There is a gift for everyone! God wants to grace each of us with gifts to live out our kingdom purposes.

Supernaturally Gifted

I was invited to a prayer group one night during my sophomore year of college. I was interested in God at that point of my life but was not overly active in my faith. There was a group of ten or so students there who were praying respectfully and unemotionally. One of them came up to me and asked if I would like to pray to receive a baptism in the Holy Spirit.

I said yes, not knowing what I was signing up for. In the moment of prayer, I felt like the love of God was filling me. I felt like God unscrewed the top of my head and poured his icy-hot presence though my whole body. I felt wholly known and wholly loved for hours. The tangible love of Jesus captured me, and on that night my whole heart and mind were drawn to focus on him.

The people in the prayer group probably thought I had lost my mind! I stood by myself with my eyes closed for hours, only capable of saying, "I love you, Jesus." Honestly, I still do not know what to theologically do with the term, "baptism in the Holy Spirit." However, I do know that God wants his love to be real to us and desires to release his gifts in our lives.

I share this story because the Spirit released the supernatural gifts in my life after this experience. It was just a matter of time before I started hearing God's voice and received the gift of tongues (heartwarming tales for another time). I also share my story because these gifts were given to me when I didn't know anyone who could disciple me through this process. How I wish a church-as-training-academy had developed me through my college years!

Not everyone will have my experience, but those who are given opportunities to experiment with their gifting within Christian community will find their contributions empowered by God. Lebron James has natural ability, but these young adults will discover *spiritual gifting*.

Spiritual gifts are the skills and abilities that are empowered by God at the moment in which they occur. God takes ordinary acts of service and uses them extraordinarily. These spiritual gifts are things we do that would be impossible without God's real presence and power.[3]

> We do not find the New Testament using *charism* (grace-inspired gifting) to indicate an enhanced or transformed natural human ability. Charism is always "a manifestation of supernatural power." Talents and charisms come to us in very different ways: talent as the result of natural

birth, and charism by a free and sovereign act of God, linked to our baptism. For this reason, talent is often a matter of heredity, but charism never.[4]

Emerging adults will discover the natural gifts they carry and the spiritual gifts that God empowers. These spiritual gifts need not look supernatural. They can be ordinary and everyday acts of service that are touched by the grace of God.

Dallas Willard once said in reference to power demonstrations:

If you try to lead the life in the Spirit by having magnificent events, you'll be a magnificent failure. Now, if you lead your life of obedience where you are expectant of the Holy Spirit to assist you to lead a life of obedience, there are going to be magnificent events, and they won't hurt you."[5]

Many of the spiritual gifts listed in Scripture come without any pizzazz at all. There are no bells and whistles or flashing lights. They are presented as natural abilities infused with God's grace, for God's purposes.[6]

Take the gift of teaching or the gift of administration as examples. These are just natural abilities, aren't they? They can be. There are non-Christian teachers. There are non-Christian administrators as well. Anyone can teach and administrate with excellence. However, when God breathes on a person's teaching, then the word of God comes to life in the hearts and minds of the hearers. This kind of teaching transforms communication of information into a manifestation of the Holy Spirit. Same for administration: God-empowered administration reveals God in a supernatural way. The same is true with any action we take that God empowers in his strength.

Charlie is a twenty-something-year-old friend who lives in my city. He works as a youth sports league organizer. He has an awesome home with plenty of space. Charlie loves to host people for parties and get-togethers. He and his wife think about how to welcome new people in their home and how they can love their community with the space that they've been given.

Their home has a front porch that women love to hang out on. The basement has a smoking parlor where men gather for long conversations and laughs. Charlie makes unbelievable beer cheese and pretzels, a mean gin and tonic, and people have to be careful not to eat too many of their homemade chocolate chip cookies covered with icing.

Charlie has been given the spiritual gift of hospitality (see 1 Peter 4:9–10). It is absolutely a supernatural gifting from God. I have eaten in their home with college students, homeless women, and refugees. Charlie makes his house available to the vulnerable and the needy.

People who visit feel included and loved. Visitors often have breakthrough moments in their relationship with God while sitting around the kitchen table or in the living room (and in the smoking parlor, if you're brave enough to believe it!). Charlie has a knack for hospitality, but the Holy Spirit has transformed his talent into a spiritual gift. Charlie's hospitality reveals Jesus to others.

That is after all what a *manifestation* of the Holy Spirit is— an act of love that reveals Jesus to others. We shared the classic 1 Corinthians 12:4–7 scripture on the spiritual gifts in the previous section. There, we are told that each person is given "the manifestation of the Spirit." Every young adult has been empowered by the Holy Spirit to serve and love others in a way that reveals Jesus. What a powerful promise! They can expect God's supernatural hand to bless them as they explore and unearth their gifting.

Service is not about any one person's ability. It is about the act of love that God illuminates to fulfill his purposes. All of the pressure is on God. This is really good news for new believers as they explore the spiritual disciplines for the first time.

Twice-Given Gifts

One final nugget from the Corinthians passage: Paul tells us that the manifestation of the Spirit is given to all for what reason? "For the *common good*" (v. 7, emphasis added). Meaning, the new gifts that young adults discover should always be used for the sake of others. In fact, *we most often discover our gifting when we serve.*

The gifts are ignited when we put faith in action. It's so practical! Think about it. If you never pray, then you'll never receive the gift of tongues. If you never teach others, then you'll never have the gift of teaching. If you don't attempt to pray for the sick, then you'll never have the gift of healing.

But, if given the opportunity and challenge to step out to lead, one just might find they have an apostolic gifting. If given the opportunity to intercede, one might discover a prophetic gifting. If asked to serve the marginalized, one might uncover a gift of hospitality.

Spiritual gifts are intended to be twice-given gifts. We are given them so that we can give them away. The spiritual gifts we receive are rarely for ourselves. They are gifts God gives us so that we can give them to others! Paul insists that gifts were granted to individuals not primarily for their own enjoyment but, rather, for the edification or "building up" of the community (1 Cor. 14:12).[7]

A Christian community that operates as a Jesus dojo can help young adults discover their spiritual gifting. It is the perfect time of life for them to explore what they are good at and how they fit into the life of the church. Remember, they are hungry to take risks and explore the raw and gritty side of faith!

That means it is on us as leaders to invite them into spaces where they can experiment and get messy. If we want them to be involved in the life of a church, then we can't just ask them to stack chairs or open doors on a Sunday morning. Twenty-somethings want to be challenged to live a real faith and to sacrifice for the sake of others.

Consider the gift lists that are in Scripture.[8] They're not comprehensive, but they are not relegated to slinging coffee or working a soundboard. The lists include things like apostleship, teaching, tongues and interpretation, miracles, faith, discerning spirits, shepherding, etc. These are radical Spirit-filled acts! Imagine your young adults moving and operating in these giftings. What would happen to your church, your city, and within their generation if they came to life in these gifts? The result would be nothing short of revival.

Emerging adults are in a prime time of life to be challenged. Forged families are the safe space for them to practice a risky faith and to discover their giftings. I gave the example of house church earlier, but there are many ways to build forged families that can work as dojos within the local church.

I love that some churches have residencies where students are trained for ministry within cohorts of trusted peers. College internships are also a great way to bring in students for training and equipping. Some churches create communities of apprentices where twenty-somethings are invited to preach, lead prayer ministry, or oversee outreach—all while walking alongside a spiritual mentor within the church.[9] Banding is another avenue for creating communities of participation and training.

There are an endless number of ways to build forged families which allow young adults to discover their giftings and contribute. You have an army of kingdom warriors in the seats of your church waiting to be activated. The only question is: Will you invite them to participate and lead?

CHAPTER TEN

Pilgrim Together

Spiritual Parenting through the Wilderness Years

Abraham himself had been sent into the wilderness, told to leave his father's house . . . this was the narrative of all generations, and that it is only by the grace of God that we are made instruments of His providence and participants in a fatherhood that is always ultimately his.
—Marilynne Robinson, *Gilead* [1]

A HOUSE CHURCH GATHERING CAN BE DISCOMFORTING. For one, others are likely to stare at you from across the living room while singing a song. For two, you are expected to talk and pray during the worship service. You will stick out like a sore thumb if you excuse yourself from group interaction. For three, children. Children are all over the place during worship. They scream. They run around. They bang toys. You are in a home. There is nowhere else for them to go. This is not the American church norm.

Most people are used to worshipping with their own generations. Children and youth are excused from the average worship service. The upside is that things are quiet and reverent. The downside is that some youth make it to emerging adulthood without any intergenerational relationships. They and their mates have grown up in a church silo. They have each other but know no one outside of their peers.

The distance between generations creates a substantial community breakdown within the local church. We have talked much about the mass exodus of emerging adults leaving the church and how family-like relationships are the anchor strong enough to embed them in the faith. Perhaps the most important family-like relationships they will ever develop are those with spiritual parents. These intergenerational relationships close the age gap and provide stability in a chaotic time.

Older Christians should be guiding North Stars for emerging adult believers who need shining examples of how to live faithfully in adulthood. They are in a disorienting stage of life and look to elders in the faith for guidance. As a leader you can help them develop the mentoring and discipling relationships that they so desperately need. This chapter will show how a forged family can break down the generational barrier that keeps people apart.

Spiritual Parenting

Spiritual parenting. I still remember the first time I heard the phrase. I was in the process of choosing small group members at my college ministry. Group selection worked a little bit like a sports draft where we took students' names off a board when chosen by a leader. On one June day there was an argument over which small group a particular student would be placed for the upcoming year. He was a popular student and a lot of different people wanted him to be in their group. At one point a selector yelled, "The student should be in my group! I'm his spiritual father!"

The phrase fell flat, and the room fell silent. Everyone went silent because none of us knew exactly what he meant by the title. Spiritual parent? What a claim! What does that mean? Championing a title like *spiritual father* or *mother* felt weighty.

The title was a trump card played to put a claim on the student, but the title left us unsure of what to think.

Spiritual father—spiritual mother—spiritual parenting. I have heard these expressions tossed around a good bit during my ten years as a campus ministry pastor. I noticed these terms piqued the interest of college students without fail. When used, the quirky little labels struck a soul resonance in the hearts of emerging adults—despite the fact that no one ever bothered to define them.

Ask a room full of students if they want a spiritual parent, and all the hands in the room will go up. The idea connects with young Christians because they feel the need for some type of older companionship. They are naturally drawn to mature Christians who can help them navigate life's journey.

Statistics show that spiritual parents do more than meet a felt need. These relationships may just be the reason that some young adults stay in the faith, while their peers exit the church. Young Christians who feel relationally connected with a mature believer are more likely to maintain their faith and live it out boldly. Research shows that most strongly committed emerging adult Christians had older friends from church while growing up. Seventy-seven percent of committed young adults claimed they had strong intergenerational ties in their faith community.[2]

The young adult desire for spiritual parents is validated by the research. People tend to wander through emerging adulthood lost and alone. They are left to explore their new adult identity without any guiding light. They long for a vision of a life worth emulating, a vision that can only be found through intergenerational relationships.

Wilderness Years

I mentioned the Pinetops Foundation study called "The Great Opportunity" in the introduction. That was a while ago (thanks for hanging through the whole journey!), so let's revisit it. This massive study projects that if current trends continue, more than one million youth in the church today will choose to leave each year for the next three decades. The church will look radically different by 2050, with twenty to forty million young adults projected to leave the church.[3]

Emerging adulthood is a wilderness. "The Great Opportunity" highlights the fact that students who grow up in church will leave high school and enter into a faith desert. No amount of nurturing in their grade school years will save them from this reality. Their faith will be tested when they leave home.

Many students grow up in a church oasis. They are surrounded by people who think from a faith perspective. Their schools, extracurriculars, and friendships might be explicitly Christian. The oasis that nourishes them reinforces a Christian worldview. There is nothing wrong with this, except that there will come a time when it is tested.

Upon high school graduation, young adult Christians walk out of their faith environments and into a new culture that brings faith into question. They do things like move cities, start college, go on gap years, and work internships. The transition is inevitable for most. In this change, they walk out of the oasis and into a broader identity desert. This desert has a name. It goes by postmodernity.

Certainly this will not be the first time our young adults have engaged with postmodern thought. As fish are unaware of the water, so we are unaware of just how pervasive relativism is in our society and our thinking. But the difference between a person's high school years and their twenties is this: each twenty-something will be challenged to explicitly affirm their belief in Jesus, on their own, and in the denial of the post-truth world that surrounds them.

Thus, people are lured into the desert where they will skeptically examine the tenants of the faith and their reason for belief.

This postmodern process of being led into the middle of nowhere is called deconstruction. Deconstruction happens when a once-held truth is brought into question.

In the wilderness, the scaffolding which once held a person upright—those pegs which secured a person in what they thought to be inherently true—are beaten away. A once-tall structure is brought down to earth when the truth scaffolding is deconstructed.

Young adult identity is leveled in the desert. The wilderness becomes a land of searching. It is a space of self-questioning. All the things that once defined a person will be challenged: their childhood beliefs, the rhythms of life they once held, and the priority of previous relationships.

The ultimate testing of faith happens when one steps into the young adult wilderness. Their sense of identity is strained. Many who were, at one time, found will lose their way in the desert, stranded and without a compass.

The Nova Effect

The transition into college is a good example of how this can happen. A student at eighteen years of age leaves their hometown, transitions to a new city, and finds themselves surrounded by new people. The student no longer feels any pressure from friends, classes, clubs, or roommates to maintain a hold onto faith. And at the same time, they are exposed to a slew of new ideologies that challenge their way of thinking.

Being exposed to new ideas is very important. Education should be pursued. The faith crisis and deconstruction problem come more so as the result of lackluster discipleship in the teen years. Most teens are not secure enough in their faith to withstand the cross pressures put on them by competing ideas at the university level. The transition into the emerging adult wilderness exposes the weakness in their personal belief.

The reality is that we live in a society where multiple world-views compete on the public stage for power and dominance. Emerging adulthood is the hotbed of this ideological struggle, where people encounter difference of opinion for the first time.

How many people go off to university to realize for the first time that not everyone thinks like them, dresses like them, or votes like them?

Encountering other belief systems is an important part of human development and is valuable in so many ways. True faith cannot thrive without exposure to other cultures and value sets. But worldview battles have a way of creeping into our thought life in the form of deconstruction. Young adults who lose themselves in this wilderness will be tempted to leave their Christian faith.

Cultural critic and philosopher Charles Taylor has a theory termed the "Nova Effect." The Nova Effect is a picture borrowed from astronomy. My dad is a big astronomy nerd, so I asked him what a supernova is. He said, "A supernova is when a star collapses in on itself, dies, and explodes into hundreds or thousands of little lights."

Christianity was the predominant worldview of generations past. Christendom was the singular light in Western society for more than a thousand years. Yet, the light of Christendom now wanes as Western culture has rejected its past. Christian worldview has imploded in on itself, and hundreds or thousands of worldviews have emerged in its place. These new belief sets are people's attempts at trying to make meaning of life in a world that no longer acknowledges transcendent or spiritual realities.[4]

Young adults will be lost to confusion—or indifference, which is even worse—when they're launched into nova array of competing lights. Each of them will have to define themselves and their lives while being bombarded with messaging that attempts to destabilize them.

Part of the Nova Effect is that you never quite feel comfortable with any particular belief set for too long because you are engulfed by other opinions. Every worldview fights for our attention in an attempt to redefine our values, our loves, and our view of the good life. Many Christians are lost in post-Christian thought, doubting what could be true.

To live in our culture today is to live in doubt; to doubt your family, to doubt your religion, to doubt your society; to doubt yourself.

Emerging adults are disoriented in this desert, looking for a guiding light, but overwhelmed by endless options. They exist in this wilderness as sojourners, those who are wandering from home without direction.

It is impossible for these sojourners to successfully navigate life and faith if they are alone in the journey and without a guiding light.

From Sojourner to Pilgrim

Sojourner is a term that we see a lot in the book of Genesis. It comes from the Hebrew word *gur*, which means to live among people who are not blood relatives.[5] Leaving family is a key element of sojourning. Sojourners are those who leave their homeland to wander the wilderness of strange and foreign lands. A sojourner's travels threatens their identity. Their sense of self is challenged after they leave their family and native home. We see this story repeated over and over again in Scripture.

Adam and Eve were exiled from their home in Eden. Cain was cast out. Abraham was called from his home. Each of them sojourned. Adam and Eve were sojourners when they were cast from their garden home. Cain was a sojourner when he was banished from his land. Abraham sojourned when he left his homeland of Ur. They were vulnerable in their sojourning, restlessly wandering and homeless.

Emerging adults are sojourners when they leave home. Their identities are shaken as they are forced to wander the identity wilderness without the familiarity of home or belonging.

And yet, *not all those who wander are lost.*[6] Scripture does provide an example of someone who wandered without losing their sense of self. Jesus was expelled into the wilderness late in his emerging adulthood. His wilderness experience was not unlike the sojourners described in the Old Testament.

But Jesus did not go into the wilderness without a strong sense of self or a clear direction. We can understand why Jesus had such a profound sense of purpose when looking at the gospel narrative leading up to his time in the desert. Luke 3:21 says:

> Now when all the people were baptized, and when Jesus also had been baptized and was praying, the heavens were opened, and the Holy Spirit descended on him in bodily form, like a dove; and a voice came from heaven, "You are my beloved Son; with you I am well pleased."

Jesus received a blessing from his Father before his wandering in the wilderness.

God the Father first spoke identity over the Son. The Father's blessing did not save him from this wandering. Jesus still had to enter the wilderness, he still had his identity tested, and he still had to face the temptations of Satan.

However, Jesus went into his wandering with a strong understanding that he belonged to the Father and came out of his wandering more empowered to live his life's call than when he entered (see Luke 4:14). The blessing of the Father transformed Jesus' journey from a sojourn to a pilgrimage.

Pilgrimage is nothing like sojourning. I have traveled worldwide on adventure trips with God. Pilgrimage is different than your average vacationing. The anticipation is heightened because it's an act of faith. You are leaving your home to seek and experience God.

Maddie's and my trip to the Holy Land is our greatest pilgrimage to date. We went with both sets of our parents. The sites were great and faith-bolstering. But the presence of our parents was as important as the locations themselves. We got to pray, worship, and explore with them along the way. The trip profoundly shaped our identity as individuals and as a couple.

Just as we saw above in the life of Jesus, the presence of a spiritual parent transforms the emerging adult journey from a sojourn into a pilgrimage. The spiritual parent stabilizes a young adult's identity in the desert. They provide a North Star and guiding light in a world of limitless options.

The truth that defined Jesus was spoken by his Father. It bolstered him in an unshakeable identity and a profound sense of purpose. It allowed him to stand firmly in truth when tempted by Satan. Jesus traveled not as a sojourner, but as a pilgrim.

A pilgrim may not escape the dangers of wandering, but they have a strong understanding of who they are, whose they are, and where they are heading. A pilgrim is a person who is on a journey blessed by God. They know their destination is a place of God's presence, belonging, and inheritance.

A sojourner is exiled but a pilgrim is sent.

A sojourner wanders confused but a pilgrim wanders in secure identity.

A sojourner is homeless but a pilgrim is headed home.

Pilgrims wander, but they wander toward an anticipated destination. Jesus, when he roamed, did so as a Son headed toward the glorious inheritance of his Father.

Ricky's Story

Doctor Ricky Moore is an Old Testament professor at Lee University in Cleveland, Tennessee. I met Ricky a year ago when I visited a student prayer group on Lee's campus. He stood out to me because the students kept referring to him as a *spiritual father*.

There are not many professors on college campuses that would receive that kind of praise or accolades from students, but Ricky has seized his God-given opportunity to bless the lives of his students. He sees his role on campus in a unique light. Ricky said, "Beyond giving grades, skills, and academic degrees to my students, I know that I am called to impart blessings and to cultivate the callings of the daughters and sons of the next generation."

Ricky radiates fatherly encouragement and empowerment for his students. He leads the Lee prayer group, which meets three times a week to pray for an hour and a half each time. Ricky spends more than four hours a week in group prayer with dozens of students. They gravitate toward him because he is a source of love and safety on a campus where more than 50 percent of the freshman self-report struggling with episodes of depression (like so many other campuses around the country).

The Lee prayer group does not reflect that statistic. It is filled with students who are confident leaders on campus. They are empowered and encouraged to pursue their callings. Ricky is a major source of their passion and power. He constantly listens to them, prays with them, and provides blessing for the pursuit of God's call in their individual lives. Ricky responded to a generation of sojourners with a father's care, and an oasis of pilgrims has emerged.

God the Father has shared spiritual parenting with older-generation Christians. They provide a sense of the Father's grace for young believers who don't feel good enough for God or for the church. They can be a source of the Father's love for those broken by life's journey.

Amidst the wilderness, a spiritual parent reminds the young adult of who they are. They affirm God's truth, not just with their words, but with their actions. Home with God is not far away when home is found with a spiritual mother or father.

Spiritual parents represent the Father's family belonging for sojourners who have forgotten whose they are and where they belong. Spiritual mothers and fathers are ambassadors and carriers of the Father's heart among his lost sheep. Henri Nouwen described how spiritual parenting impacts younger Christians:

> As the Father, I have to carry the responsibility of a spiritually adult person and dare to trust that the real joy and real fulfillment can only come from welcoming home those who have been hurt and wounded on their life's journey, and loving them with a love that neither asks nor expects anything in return.[7]

Transforming Sojourners

Your forged family is the perfect place for wandering sojourners to be loved and blessed by you and other spiritual parents. Elder generations can transform a young adult's journey into a pilgrimage by building relationship with them. As a leader in Christian community, you have the opportunity to be their North Star in the desert.

But at this point you might be wondering how you actually begin building deep relationships with people younger than you. What does it practically look like to be a spiritual parent? I think we get some clues from the apostle Paul in his letter to the Corinthians:

> I do not write these things to make you ashamed, but to admonish you as my beloved children. For though you have countless guides in Christ, you do not have many fathers. For I became your father in Christ Jesus through the gospel. I urge you, then, be imitators of me. That is why I sent you Timothy, my beloved and faithful child in the Lord, to remind you of my ways in Christ, as I teach them everywhere in every church. (1 Cor. 4:14–17)

Paul referred to himself in this passage as a father to both
Timothy and to the Corinthian church. He is a *spiritual father*,
or a *father in the gospel*, to the Corinthians. Paul even goes so far
as to distinguish himself from the *guides* that people have in the
faith. Guidance is part of spiritual parenting but is not the most
important part. We pick up from this passage three distinct ways
that this spiritual parenting is lived out.

Home

Home is the first element of spiritual parenting that we pick up
from this passage. We should not mistake this for a physical house.
By home, we mean a place of belonging. A spiritual parent will
have relational space to include, love, and care for younger people.

Paul invited both Timothy and the Corinthians into his life.
He was relationally available to them. Timothy came alongside
him in both life and ministry. Nothing means more to a weary
sojourner than a safe space to lay their head and rest. Our young
adults need safe and trusted relationships for vulnerable and
honest life conversations.

Rob is a well-to-do bachelor in his early fifties. Never married,
he has the time and resources to care for people who have nowhere
else to turn. Rob is a small business owner who likes to employ
young men who are down-and-out on their luck. He provides
housing for some of the young men as well.

Rob has recently taken in a young man whose mom is battling
schizophrenia. She is violent and creates an unsafe environment
for him to live in. Rob stepped in and offered the young man a
place to live. He now has a safe place to stay and a father figure.
It's Rob's relational availability that makes him a safe place for
healing in the midst of sojourning. He has discipled countless
young men who have found themselves in similar situations in
the last ten years. While Rob doesn't have biological children,

he has led multiple young men to faith and become a spiritual parent to many.

Teaching

Teaching is the second element of spiritual parenting. Paul taught Timothy the way of Jesus. He taught Timothy his gospel. In the book of First Corinthians, Paul has commissioned Timothy to teach that same gospel to the Corinthians. We don't need to look for great theologians to be spiritual parents, but we do need older mentors who bring to life the basic truths of Scripture. This is a unique kind of teaching that is necessary for every young Christian to receive.

Teaching in a trusted relationship is much different than the type of instruction I am giving you through this book. I am teaching you from hundreds, if not thousands, of miles away. You may feel that you know me from the stories I have shared, but we have never actually met. This is true for the teaching that takes place from the stage in many churches. Much of the teaching that we sit under on Sunday morning is given from people that we do not actually know. It is teaching without relationship. Preachers do what I am doing now. I'm giving you information. I hope that it's helpful, but the instruction that happens in spiritual parenting, instruction from relationship, is much more effective.

Truth-telling and theology sharing is an indispensable element of spiritual parenting. But spiritual parents teach from a sense of home—a place of belonging—making them powerful instructors. Teaching within the confines of a trusted and loving relationship is much more effective than a word shared in a book or from a stage.

Paul taught Timothy and the Corinthians from a place of relational authority. He had already demonstrated his care and love to the people he was teaching. They had seen his care firsthand. The title of *spiritual father* wasn't given freely, it was hard-earned through love, care, and sacrifice.

There is an old cheesy axiom that says: "They won't care how much you know until they know how much you care." Listening is the superpower of spiritual parenting that shows that you care. You cannot skip over listening. Young adults won't want to hear your advice—no matter how correct or how spiritual it is—if they are first not heard. However, the opposite is true as well. Listen long enough, and you'll see the doors swing wide open for emerging adults to receive what you have to share.

Demonstration

Finally, the third element of spiritual parenting is *demonstration*. Paul urged the Corinthians to imitate his life! "Mentoring is not an institution to manage—it is a lifestyle to emulate."[8] This is undoubtedly why he sent Timothy to the Corinthians. Paul said it explicitly: "I urge you to imitate me. For this reason I have sent to you Timothy . . ." (1 Cor. 4:16–17a NIV). Timothy spent time with Paul.

Timothy learned the way and rhythm of Jesus by observing how Paul lived his life. He saw the way Paul conducted his faith in every area: family, business, and ministry. In this passage we now see that Timothy is charged to pass on this lifestyle to the church in Corinthians. Paul didn't just send a letter to the Corinthians; he sent a messenger with the letter, someone to demonstrate what he has modeled.

In the same way, we should open up our lives for emerging adults to witness us live out the way of Jesus in every area. They don't just want a place to belong, but a lifestyle to follow. This runs much deeper than a Bible study at Starbucks. Offer more to them than detached theology. Invite them over to cook meals or do woodworking. Let them see how you interact with your family and love your spouse. This creates within them a vision for what life can be. It helps to set a destination for their pilgrimage.

Lewis is a sixty-five-year-old man who lives in a subdivision with his wife. He has three grown kids who are out of the house. Lewis carries around a fire of evangelism for his neighborhood and for emerging generations. He and his wife host everyone on their street for dinner twice a year. He is always scheming about ways to engage his neighbors with the gospel. One of the couples on his street recently wanted to purchase a home. Lewis is a real estate agent. He helped them with all the ins and outs of home-buying free of charge.

Over the course of time they have seen Lewis's relationship with his wife, interacted with him around the neighborhood, witnessed his business practices, and now have received life advice. This is the kind of relational development required to build a spiritual parenting relationship. The doors will eventually swing open for Lewis to lead them in faith as well.

Common Interest

At this point you might be thinking: *Spiritual parenting is outside of my reach! I could never be a Rob or a Lewis!*

Might I politely disagree?

Spiritual parenting isn't for the super-Christian. Neither Rob nor Lewis is a professional pastor. They never have been and never will be. They have no professional Christian training. They aren't theologians or Bible experts.

And no, they are not cool. They don't look like Bono. They don't wear skinny jeans or play rock music. They are average men in their fifties and sixties. Nothing more, nothing less.

There's nothing outwardly spectacular about them . . . except for the way they intentionally form relationships. They have provided both a home and a sense of belonging for weary sojourners in the journey of emerging adulthood. Anyone with relational availability can do that. That's truly all it takes to begin taking in the spiritually homeless. Think about the older people you were close to who impacted your faith when you were in college and your early twenties. Were they spiritual giants? Were they cool? My guess is: probably not.

We need to break the stigma that it's only the cool and the trained who can impact emerging generations. That's simply not true. The people who had the greatest impact on my life in those years were the available.

Available people have made the difference in my life. These people created space and invited me into their lives. Conor was available to me. He was a man of about forty years old who asked me to get lunch every week. I am so thankful for Conor. He was a stable presence for me in the middle of a tumultuous time.

I also think of my eighty-year-old grandpa who called me every week to talk sports and faith. Or an older lady named Julie, who invited me over for some killer grilled cheese and would inevitably pray for me during lunch. These were the people who impacted my life in emerging adulthood. They provided a sense of home and belonging. They gave me a vision of how God could use my life in the future.

I still want to emulate their lives, and they weren't the cool or the trained. They were the available. The ones who provided home. They were the ones God used to transform my journey.

And now, to close this book, I leave you with the first step of building a forged family: invite one young adult into your life. You do not need to be cool, only available. You do not need to be a great teacher, only a loving a presence. Open yourself to relationship and intentionally invite a young adult into your life. Provide them with a sense of home, teach with your words and your love, demonstrate the way of Jesus to them.

Your forged family starts with your spiritual parenting. If you can model family-like belonging for one sojourner, then a culture of belonging can be set and others will follow.

CONCLUSION

ARTHUR WALLIS ONCE SUGGESTED THAT WE HINDER revival by overlooking failure within the church. There are some who want to continue with church as normal, despite the fact that we live in a time of spiritual crisis. The surrounding signs show us that major change needs to take place within church culture in the Western world. Gen Zers and Millennials are exiting the faith by the hundreds of thousands, the pandemic crisis has accelerated church deterioration, and many key faith leaders are being exposed as fraudulent. If we remain in our current patterns, then we will lose emerging generations.

This is not a moment to lower our heads and tread forward without repentance. It is also not a moment for us to cower with fear and trepidation. Rather, this moment—our moment—is a time for us to turn to God with expectancy and ask: What will church renewal and a fresh Great Awakening look like in our day?

God is not caught off guard by the occurrences of our time; he holds all things in his hands. One day Jesus will return, but he will not be greeted by a whimpering church. His coming will be welcomed by a radiant and victorious bride. We see evidence of this happening around the world as Christianity is spreading like wildfire in the global south. If God has moved in power in our past and in our present world, why would we not expect God to revive emerging adults and church within the West?

The young adult problem is not beyond God's reach or touch. This time of church recession is not a time for mourning. It is a time for renewal. It is a time for fresh innovation and for purity of faith. God is using this time to prepare his church for the next revival.

Many leaders feel that the Western church stands at the precipice of a great opportunity. The Spirit is speaking to those of us whose hearts are soft and ears are open. And renewal expressions are now emerging out of this desperate season. Some call for a return to liturgy, others for corporate intercession, and there are those who champion countercultural spiritual rhythms. I feel kindred to these leaders and these efforts toward change.

Yet, there is a singular ailment at the center of our cultural, church, and emerging generation decline. That ailment is individualism. It goes by many names: loneliness, isolation, selfishness, greed, etc. And its symptoms are depression, anxiety, and all forms of breakdown within our civil institutions—churches included.

In the midst of this breakdown, there is another point of renewal that we cannot miss as church leaders and committed disciples of Jesus. That point is the renewal of family-like community within our congregations.

This point sat burning within my gut as I wrote. And I pray that it now sits burning within yours as well.

My hope for you is twofold in the closing of this book. My first hope is that you have fallen in love with the potential of forged families. The young adult crisis is a relational crisis. They desperately need Jesus, and they desperately need spiritual friendship. Forged families can connect them to both. Wield its power and God may heal your church along with its twenty-somethings. You now have the tools to build deep and intimate community where young adults can journey toward God together.

My second hope is that you now see emerging generations in a new light. Most leaders have been in the dark, opting to focus their ministries on youth and established families. But you are different. You now know emerging adults—their aches, struggles, hopes, lifestyle, and spirituality. Lead them with confidence and serve them with empathy.

I am full of faith that God will use you to forge family with the young adults in your life. So I urge you: Do not stay still. Do not resist change. Do not continue with church-as-normal. You sit at the precipice of a great opportunity. God is moving you, and the road to renewal runs through community.

GLOSSARY

Authenticity: The cultural value of expressing feeling and inner realities in identity formation and projection. The authentic self is found within a person, not without. See *expressive individualism*. This concept is borrowed from Charles Taylor.

Bands: Groups of three to five people who gather regularly for Christian encouragement, discernment, and accountability.

Choice Anxiety: The stress that most emerging adults feel when they are presented with endless options and choices for identity formation. The key areas of question are vocation, location, and spouse.

Deconstruction: The process that many young adults experience, within their emerging adult identity formation, of taking apart their childhood faith one tenant at a time to doubt and critique that belief. This happens when the identity foreman tears down the identity structure of their childhood faith.

Digital Farming: The role pastors take on when church goes online. Pastors feel pressure to cultivate followers for views, likes, and comments. They harvest eyeball minutes.

Emerging Adulthood: A recently developed life stage of people ages eighteen to twenty-nine characterized by learning in higher education, delayed marriage, frequent job and career changes, and the delay of child raising.[1] I use the term broadly in this writing to encompass young adults within the Millennial and Gen Z generations who are thirty and younger.

Emerging Adult Wilderness: The landscape of identity formation that young adults experience. They are encouraged to build a sense of self without any help or assistance from the outside. They are presented with many options for belief in this wilderness and are largely without guidance.

Expressive Individualism: We each create our own identity by expressing our inner reality through choice and action. Identity cannot be given or received. This concept is borrowed from Charles Taylor.

Forged Family: Intimate communities of emerging adult Christians who weld together within the fires of emerging adulthood to support one another, practice the spiritual disciplines, and worship. The quality, rhythms, and bond of their relationships can only accurately be described by using the word *family*.

Gen Zers: People born between 1995 and 2012 are part of Generation Z.

Identity Foreman: Young adults feel pressure to construct their own identity from the ground up, without help or inheritance from family, tradition, society, or religion. Their construction materials include consumer choices, outward actions, and digital image projection.

Millennials: People born between 1980 and 1995 are part of the Millennial generation.

Pilgrim: A young adult who goes through the emerging adult wilderness with the blessing of a spiritual parent.

Separation Anxiety: The stress that sets in when emerging adults consistently view the stable adult life they desire via social media and apps. They are driven in their stage of life to close the gap between young adulthood and the established adulthood (characterized by the "American dream").

Sojourner: A young adult who goes through the questions of the emerging adult wilderness lost and alone.

Spiritual Parent: An elder Christian who relationally creates a sense of home for emerging adult Christians and, in doing so, both teaches and demonstrates to them the basics of the Christian faith.

Young Adults/Emerging Adults: People ages eighteen to twenty-nine are in this category.

Young Adult Exodus: The big problem that the church faces of young adults exiting the faith by the millions. The Pinetops Foundation study, "The Great Opportunity," details this problem, as described in the introduction.

The Way of Jesus: A term popularized by John Mark Comer that invites people into the discipleship process, learning to do the things that Jesus taught and modeled. Those who practice the way of Jesus practice the spiritual disciplines in an attempt to live the Christian life.

NOTES

Introduction

1. Quoted in Rod Dreher, *The Benedict Strategy: A Strategy for Christians in a Post-Christian Nation* (New York, NY: Penguin Random House, 2017), 8.
2. "The Great Opportunity: The American Church in 2050," Pinetops Foundation, 2018, https://www.greatopportunity.org/.
3. I copied this term from a David Brooks article where he, in turn, credited an academic named David Burns with the term *forged family*. David Brooks, "The Nuclear Family Was a Mistake," *The Atlantic*, March 2020; https://www.theatlantic.com/magazine/archive/2020/03/the-nuclear-family-was-a-mistake/605536/.

Chapter One
The Wall of Identity: Building Yourself from Scratch

1. "Major Depression: The Impact on Overall Health," BlueCross BlueShield, May 10, 2018, https://www.bcbs.com/sites/default/files/file-attachments/health-of-america-report/HoA_Major_Depression_Report.pdf.
2. "Major Depression," National Institute of Major Health, 2020, https://www.nimh.nih.gov/health/statistics/major-depression.
3. B. Janet Hibbs and Anthony Rostain, *The Stressed Years of Their Lives: Helping Your Kid Survive and Thrive During Their College Years* (New York, NY: St. Martin's Press, 2019), 149.
4. "New Cigna Study Reveals Loneliness at Epidemic Levels in America," Cigna, May 1, 2018, https://www.multivu.com/players/English/8294451-cigna-us-loneliness-survey/.

5. Hibbs and Rostain, *The Stressed Years of Their Lives*, 9.

6. James K. A. Smith, *How (Not) to Be Secular: Reading Charles Taylor* (Grand Rapids, MI: Wm. B. Eerdmans Publishing Co., 2014), 141.

7. Joseph H. Hellerman, *When the Church Was a Family: Recapturing Jesus' Vision for Authentic Christian Community* (Nashville, TN: B&H Academic, 2009), 22.

8. Christian Smith and Patricia Snell, *Souls in Transition: The Religious and Spiritual Lives of Emerging Adults* (New York, NY: Oxford University Press, 2009), 45.

9. Charles Taylor, *A Secular Age* (Cambridge, MA, and London, England: The Belknap Press of Harvard University Press, 2007), 475. Taylor gives this definition of authenticity: "The understanding of life which emerges with the Romantic expressivism of the late-eighteenth century, that each one of us has his/her own way of realizing our humanity, and that it is important to find and live out one's own, as against surrendering to conformity with a model imposed on us from outside, by society, or the previous generation, or religious or political authority."

10. Joshua McNall, *Long Story Short: The Bible in Six Simple Movements* (Franklin, TN: Seedbed Publishing, 2018), 28.

11. Hellerman, *When the Church Was a Family*, 130.

Chapter Two
The Wall of Distraction: Detoxing from Medi(a)cation

1. Sherry Turkle, *Alone Together: Why We Expect More from Technology and Less from Each Other* (New York, NY: Basic Books, 2017), 227.

2. J. Ellsworth Kalas, *Preaching in an Age of Distraction* (Downers Grove, IL: InterVarsity Press, 2014), 17.

3. Turkle, *Alone Together*, 262.

4. Patrick J. Deenan, *Why Liberalism Failed* (New Haven, CT: Yale University Press, 2019), 15.

5. Jean M. Twenge, *iGen: Why Today's Super-Connected Kids Are Growing Up Less Rebellious, More Tolerant, Less Happy—and Completely Unprepared for Adulthood* (New York, NY: Atria Paperback, 2017), 51.

6. Ibid., 71–81.

7. Ronald Rohlheiser, *The Shattered Lantern: Rediscovering a Felt Presence of God* (New York, NY: The Crossroad Publishing Co., 2013), 134.

8. Brené Brown, *Daring Greatly: How the Courage to Be Vulnerable Transforms the Way We Live, Love, Parent, and Lead* (New York, NY: Avery, 2012), 176.

9. C. S. Lewis, *Mere Christianity* (New York, NY: Harper Collins, 1952), 136–37.

10. Andy Crouch, *The Tech-Wise Family: Everyday Steps for Putting Technology in Its Proper Place* (Grand Rapids, MI: BakerBooks, 2017), 145.

11. Kalas, *Preaching in an Age of Distraction,* 32.

12. Turkle, *Alone Together,* 161.

13. *Parks and Rec,* season 5, episode 8, "Pawnee Commons."

14. Alan Noble, *Disruptive Witness: Speaking Truth in a Distracted Age* (Downers Grove, IL: IVP Books, 2018), Kindle.

15. Ruth Haley Barton, *Sacred Rhythms: Arranging Our Lives for Spiritual Transformation* (Downers Grove, IL: InterVarsity Press, 2006), 32.

16. Dietrich Bonhoeffer, *Life Together: The Classic Exploration of Christian Community* (New York, NY: HarperOne, 1954), 77.

17. Henri J. M. Nouwen, *Reaching Out: The Three Movements of the Spiritual Life* (New York, NY: Doubleday, 1975), 42.

Chapter Three
The Wall of Competition
Competing in the Social Media Arena

1. Regina Luttrell and Karen McGrath, *The Millennial Mindset: Unraveling Fact from Fiction* (Lanham, MD: Rowman & Littlefield, 2015), 76.

2. Jean M. Twenge, *iGen: Why Today's Super-Connected Kids Are Growing Up Less Rebellious, More Tolerant, Less Happy—and Completely Unprepared for Adulthood* (New York, NY: AtriaPaperback, 2017), 78.

3. "Social Media Fact Sheet," Pew Research Center, https://www.pewresearch.org/internet/fact-sheet/social-media/.

4. Cal Newport, *Digital Minimalism: Choosing a Focused Life in a Noisy World* (New York, NY: Portfolio/Penguin, 2019), 34.

5. Andy Crouch, *The Tech-Wise Family: Everyday Steps for Putting Technology in Its Proper Place* (Downers Grove, IL: BakerBooks, 2017), 96.

6. Richard Plass and James Cofield, *The Relational Soul: Moving from False Self to Deep Connection* (Downers Grove, IL: InterVarsity Press, 2014), 66.

7. https://www.sciencedaily.com/releases/2021/03/210308111852.htm.

8. Jonathan Sacks, *Morality: Restoring the Common Good in Divided Times* (New York, NY: Basic Books, 2020), e-book.

9. https://www.nytimes.com/2021/03/05/opinion/influencers-glennon-doyle-instagram.html.

10. Mark Sayers, *Disappearing Church: From Cultural Relevance to Gospel Resilience* (Chicago, IL: Moody Publishers, 2016), 59.

11. Tim Elmore's *Generation Z Unfiltered: Facing Nine Hidden Challenges of the Most Anxious Population* has a couple of very helpful chapters on the fluidity of Gen Z individual identity and the reintegration of the self.

12. Dallas Willard, *The Spirit of the Disciplines: Understanding How God Changes Lives* (New York, NY: Harper One, 1988), 179.

Chapter 4
The Wall of Self-Sufficiency
Bridging the Gap between Your Capacity and Calling

1. Andrew Van Dam, "The Unluckiest Generation in U.S. History: Millennials have faced the worst economic odds, and many will never recover," *The Washington Post*, https://www.washington

post.com/business/2020/05/27/millennial-recession-covid/, June 5, 2020.

2. Fyodor Dostoyevsky, *The Brothers Karamazov* (Mineola, NY: Dover Publications, 2005), 276, emphasis mine.

3. Regina Luttrell and Karen McGrath, *The Millennial Mindset: Unraveling Fact from Fiction* (Lanham, MD: Rowman & Littlefield, 2015), 94.

4. Jean M. Twenge, *iGen: Why Today's Super-Connected Kids Are Growing Up Less Rebellious, More Tolerant, Less Happy—and Completely Unprepared for Adulthood* (New York, NY: AtriaPaperback, 2017), 195.

5. Christian Smith and Patricia Snell, *Souls in Transition: The Religious and Spiritual Lives of Emerging Adults* (New York, NY: Oxford University Press, 2009), 34–35.

6. Andrew Roberts, *Churchill: Walking with Destiny* (New York, NY: Penguin Books, 2018), 35.

7. Richard Plass and James Cofield, *The Relational Soul: Moving from False Self to Deep Connection* (Downers Grove, IL: InterVarsity Press, 2014), 65, emphasis mine.

8. Ibid., 12.

9. Kyle Martin, "Brutally Honest Valedictorian Regrets Being the Top of the Class," The King's Academy, West Palm Beach, FL, May, 31 2019, https://www.youtube.com/watch?v=T76FdtKreNQ.

Chapter 5
The Wall of Transition
Being Steady to Root Faith

1. Jon Tyson, *Sacred Roots: Why the Church Still Matters* (Grand Rapids, MI: Zondervan, Barna Group, 2013), Kindle.

2. Heather Long, "The New Normal: 4 Job Changes by the Time You're 32," CNN Business, Apr. 12, 2016, https://money.cnn.com/2016/04/12/news/economy/millennials-change-jobs-frequently/index.html.

3. Amy Adkins, "Millennials: The Job-Hopping Generation," *Gallup Business Journal*, https://www.gallup.com/workplace /231587/millennials-job-hopping-generation.aspx.

4. Robert Putnam, *Bowling Alone: The Collapse and Revival of American Community* (New York, NY: Simon and Schuster Paperbacks, 2000), 205.

5. Pete Greig, comments made during his contribution to the Awakening Project, May 20, 2021.

6. Wendell Berry, *Jayber Crow* (Berkeley, CA: Counterpoint, 2000), 72.

7. Bauman Zygmunt, *Liquid Love* (Cambridge, UK: Polity Press, 2003), Kindle.

8. Tyson, *Sacred Roots*, Kindle.

Chapter 6
Belong Together
What Grabs Your Attention Grabs Your Affection

1. Gordon D Fee, *Paul, Spirit, and the People of God.* (Grand Rapids, MI: Baker Academic, 1996), 75.

2. Joseph H. Hellerman, *When the Church Was a Family: Recapturing Jesus' Vision for Authentic Christian Community* (Nashville, TN: B&H Academic, 2009), 21.

3. "Practicing the Way of Jesus" is a term popularized by John Mark Comer. This language and spiritual formation paradigm appears to be a distilled version of Dallas Willard's work that has been repackaged for emerging adults to access and use. Practicing the Way teaching materials are an invaluable resource for any pastor working with emerging adults.

4. Gerhard Lohfink, *Jesus and Community* (Philadelphia, PA: Fortress Press, 1984), 122.

5. Cal Newport, *Digital Minimalism: Choosing a Focused Life in a Noisy World* (New York, NY: Portfolio/Penguin, 2019), 216.

6. James K. A. Smith, *Desiring the Kingdom: Worship, Worldview, and Cultural Formation* (Grand Rapids, MI: Baker Academic,

2009), 115–17. My thoughts on the formational dynamics of university sports culture were spurred by Smith's thoughts on "Fresher's Week" at university. I would highly recommend further reading on this concept in his work.

7. John Wesley's oft-quoted line, "The gospel of Christ knows no religion but social; no holiness but social holiness," refers the importance of community in the journey of growing in Christ. See Kevin Watson's blog post: "Wesley Didn't Say It: 'Personal and Social Holiness,'" https://kevinmwatson.com/2013/05/20 /wesley-didnt-say-it-personal-and-social-holiness.

Chapter 7
Gather Together
Zoom—The New Noise of Emerging Adult Ministries

1. Jonathan Grant, *Divine Sex: A Compelling Vision for Christian Relationships in a Hypersexualized Age* (Grand Rapids, MI: Brazos Press, 2015), Kindle.

2. Sherry Turkle, *Alone Together: Why We Expect More from Technology and Less from Each Other* (New York, NY: Basic Books, 2017), 231.

3. Jay Kim, *Analog Church: Why We Need Real People, Places, and Things in the Digital Age* (Downers Grove, IL: IVP, 2020), Kindle.

4. David Kinnaman and Mark Matlock, *Faith for Exiles: 5 Way for a New Generation to Follow Jesus in Digital Babylon* (Grand Rapids, MI: Baker Books, 2019), 43.

5. Dallas Willard, *The Divine Conspiracy: Rediscovering Our Hidden Life With God* (Harper Collins e-books), Kindle.

6. Randy Clark and Mary Healy, *The Spiritual Gifts Handbook: Using Your Gifts to Build the Kingdom* (Bloomington, MN: Chosen, 2018), 23.

7. https://www.nytimes.com/interactive/2020/07/03/us/george -floyd-protests-crowd-size.html.

8. Justin Worland, "The Overdue Awakening," *Time*, June 22 / June 29, 2020 issue.

9. "Of Whitefield it was said that by merely pronouncing the word 'Mesopotamia,' he evoked tears in his audience"; Neil Postman, *Amusing Ourselves to Death: Public Discourse in the Age of Show Business* (London: Penguin Books, 1985), 54.

Chapter 8
Band Together
168 Community

1. J. R. R. Tolkien, *The Fellowship of the Ring: Being the First Part of The Lord of the Rings.* (Boston, MA: Houghton Mifflin Company, 2004), 131.

2. Mark Sayers, *Reappearing Church: The Hope for Renewal in the Rise of Our Post Christian Culture* (Chicago, IL: Moody Publishers, 2019), 68.

3. Susie East and Ben Tinker, "How to Think Straight in the Age of Information Overload." CNN Health, Oct. 9, 2015, https://www.cnn.com/2015/10/09/health/information-overload-daniel -levitin/index.ht.

4. Joseph H. Hellerman, *When the Church Was a Family: Recapturing Jesus' Vision for Authentic Christian Community* (Nashville, TN: B&H Academic, 2009), 169.

5. M. Robert Mulholland Jr., *Invitation to a Journey: A Roadmap for Spiritual Formation* (Downers Grove, IL: InterVarsity Press), Kindle.

6. Kevin M. Watson and Scott T. Kisker, *The Band Meeting: Rediscovering Relational Discipleship in Transformational Community* (Franklin, TN: Seedbed, 2017), 77.

Chapter 9
Serve Together
Training Warriors in Their Twice-Given Gifts

1. Henri J. M. Nouwen, *Life of the Beloved: Spiritual Living in a Secular World* (New York, NY: Crossroad Publishing Company, 1992), 109.
2. Check out Mark Scandrette's *Practicing the Way of Jesus: Life Together in the Kingdom of Love* for a deep-dive of excellent thought around church-as-dojo for the spiritual practices.
3. There are many different Greek words used in Scripture that are translated into "gift" and are associated with the spiritual gifts.

> Scripture uses a rich vocabulary to describe the charisms. In 1 Corinthians 12:1–7 Paul uses no less than five terms. He calls them "spiritual gifts" (*penumatika*, literally "spirituals") because they are given by the Holy Spirit (*pneuma*). They are "charisms" because they are given freely. They are "different kinds of service" because their purpose is to serve others. They are "different kinds of working" because every time we use a gift, the Holy Spirit Himself is working through us. And they are "manifestations of the Spirit" because they make the presence of the Holy Spirit evident to others. The letter to the Hebrews uses yet another term: They are "distributions of the Holy Spirit" (Hebrews 2:4, literal translation) because the Spirit distributes them in different measure to different members of the Church.

> Extract from Randy Clark and Mary Healy, *The Spiritual Gifts Handbook: Using Your Gifts to Build the Kingdom* (Bloomington, MN: Chosen, 2018), 24.

4. Raniero Cantalamessa, *Come, Creator Spirit: Meditations on the Veni Creator* (Collegeville, MN: The Liturgical Press, 2003), 174.
5. Dallas Willard *Life in the Spirit, Session 1* (Long Beach, CA 2012). https://thegardenlb.sermon.net/main/main/10254764.

6. Dallas Willard was also known for defining grace as: "Grace is God acting in your life to accomplish what you can't accomplish on your own."

7. Robert J. Banks, *Paul's Idea of Community: The Early House Churches in Their Cultural Setting* (Grand Rapids, MI: Baker Academic, 1994), 99.

8. One can find the gift lists in the New Testament in these passages: Romans 12:6–8; 1 Corinthians 12:7–11, 28–30; and Ephesians 4:11.

9. In this statement I am thinking of Asbury Church in Madison, Alabama; The Woodlands Church in Woodlands, Texas; and G2 in York, United Kingdom.

Chapter 10
Pilgrim Together
Spiritual Parenting through the Wilderness Years

1. Marilynne Robinson, *Gilead* (New York, NY: Picador, 2004), 129.

2. David Kinnaman and Mark Matlock, *Faith for Exiles: 5 Ways for a New Generation to Follow Jesus in Digital Babylon* (Grand Rapids, MI: BakerBooks, 2019), 37.

3. "The Great Opportunity: The American Church in 2050," Pinetops Foundation, 2018, https://www.greatopportunity.org/.

4. James K. A. Smith, *How (Not) To Be Secular: Reading Charles Taylor* (Grand Rapids, MI: Wm. B. Eerdmans Publishing Co., 2014), 142.

5. R. Laird Harris, Gleason L. Archer Jr., and Bruce K. Waltke, *Theological Wordbook of the Old Testament* (Chicago, IL: The Moody Bible Institute of Chicago, 1981), 155.

6. J. R. R. Tolkien, *The Fellowship of the Ring* (New York, NY: Houghton Mifflin Co., 2004), 213.

7. Henri J. M. Nouwen, *The Return of the Prodigal Son: A Story of Homecoming* (New York, NY: Doubleday, 1992), 132.

8. Alvin L. Reid and George G. Robinson, *WITH: A Practical Guide to Informal Mentoring and Intentional Disciple Making* (Lexington, KY: Rainer Publishing, 2016), 27.

Glossary

1. These four determining markers come from Christian Smith and Patricia Snell's *Souls in Transition: The Religious and Spiritual Lives of Emerging Adults* (New York, NY: Oxford University, 2009), 4–5.

CPSIA information can be obtained
at www.ICGtesting.com
Printed in the USA
LVHW050950150623
749399LV00001B/6